FOR JUDY, WHO GAVE ME ROOTS
AND WINGS.

CONTENTS

Rustic Farmhouse SLOW COOKER

75 HANDS-OFF RECIPES FOR HEARTY, HOMESTYLE MEALS

ALLI KELLEY

Creator of Longbourn Farm

PAGE STREET
PUBLISHING CO.

PAGE STREET
PUBLISHING CO.

First published in 2020 by
Page Street Publishing Co.
27 Congress Street, Suite 105
Salem, MA 01970
www.pagestreetpublishing.com

Distributed by Macmillan, sales in Canada by The Canadian Manda Group.

24   23   22   21   20   1   2   3   4   5

ISBN-13: 978-1-64567-188-6
ISBN-10: 1-64567-188-7

Library of Congress Control Number: 2019957332

Cover and book design by Meg Baskis for Page Street Publishing Co.
Photography by Alli Kelley

Printed and bound in the United States

INTRODUCTION

I am so excited to share all the recipes in this cookbook with you! I have always loved making dinner in my slow cooker. It's an easy way to create amazing meals with one dish and have them ready and waiting for you at the end of the day.

I specifically remember trying multiple slow cooker recipes after I was first married that were no good. The food was bland, the flavors were muddled, and the recipes always called for canned soups or packets of this or that, which I never had on hand. Since then, I've developed many of my own homemade slow cooker recipes, most of which are in this book!

After those first few disastrous recipes in the slow cooker, I worked on my own to figure out how I could layer flavors so that dishes came out tasting amazing—not bland. While I was developing recipes for this cookbook, I worked hard to help you learn how to do the same. A lot of the recipes in this book use fresh herbs. Using fresh herbs will transform your cooking. They are a game changer, especially in slow cooker meals.

These recipes are rustic, because they use simple, everyday ingredients. They are things we commonly have in our farmhouse and can raise or grow on our farm. The ingredients will be easy for you to find, and you might even be inspired to grow some of them yourself!

I also love that most of these recipes feed a lot of people. Food is about family and friends at our house. Food helps us create special moments that become treasured memories. The recipes in this book can help you create the same magic around the dinner table in your home.

This cookbook is packed with recipes that everyone will love—adults as well as kids. They are flavorful but approachable and familiar. Many of them are easy to throw together and require very little prep or finish work. This means more time doing what you enjoy with those you love most, and that's what life is all about!

FAMILY FAVORITE BEEF RECIPES

On our farm we raise our own beef, which means we often have an entire steer in our freezer. I've had to learn how to use all the different cuts of beef and have experimented to determine how each cut is best prepared. At first, I always had more roasts than I knew what to do with! But over time, I understood how every cut is different and which recipes best suited each one.

Beef is one of our favorite proteins, and I know you and your family will love these recipes as much as we do. These are the recipes that cross our table most. They have filled and nourished countless people and have offered comfort and love in the same bite. One of my favorite things about cooking beef is that there is usually extra to take to a friend who needs a little boost to their day or for someone who needs a soft chair and a warm meal with our family for the night.

The slow cooker is perfect for preparing beef. You can use almost any cut of beef; they are quite easy to prepare in the slow cooker and turn out incredible every time. These recipes are packed with flavor that is layered in, so nothing tastes muddled.

Strong herbs like sage, thyme and oregano stand up well to beef's strong flavor as well as the long cooking times required in a slow cooker. Finishing off the recipes with a sprinkling of fresh herbs does wonders for slow-cooked recipes—it brightens up and reinforces all the flavors in the dish.

SAGE AND THYME CHUCK ROAST WITH VEGETABLES

This is a classic meal we love to eat for Sunday dinner. It's a wonderfully filling and satisfying meal, and it's so easy to prepare. I just add the ingredients to the slow cooker base the night before, keep it in the fridge and then pop it in the slow cooker before church. We take our Sabbath day of rest seriously at our house, and this is the perfect meal for getting a nap in while it cooks!

I prefer to use small potatoes for this roast; I like the way they keep their texture better than diced potatoes. They stay nice and creamy instead of getting grainy. Chuck roast is my favorite cut for this meal, but a round roast will work as well.

Yield: **6–8 SERVINGS**

2 tbsp (30 ml) olive oil

2–3 lb (908 g–1.4 kg) beef chuck roast

1 tsp salt

½ tsp pepper

2 medium yellow onions, quartered

4 carrots, sliced

3 lb (1.4 kg) baby or fingerling potatoes

1 cup (240 ml) beef broth

3 tbsp (45 ml) Worcestershire sauce

1 tbsp (15 ml) soy sauce

4 sage leaves, plus additional, minced, for serving

3 sprigs thyme, plus additional, minced, for serving

In a large nonstick skillet, heat the olive oil over high heat. Season the roast with the salt and pepper, rubbing it into the meat. Sear both sides of the roast in the skillet, 3 to 5 minutes per side. Set the roast aside. Place the onions, carrots and potatoes in the bottom of the slow cooker. Place the seared roast on top of the root vegetables. Pour the beef broth, Worcestershire sauce and soy sauce over the roast. Place the sage leaves and thyme sprigs in the slow cooker.

Cook the roast and vegetables on high for 4 hours or low for 8 hours. The vegetables should be tender, and the roast should be falling apart. Shred the beef with two forks and serve topped with additional minced sage and thyme.

HOMEMADE MISSISSIPPI POT ROAST

If you need a recipe to please a picky eater, a crowd or even a date, this is the recipe you want to use! It's a favorite of everyone who tries it, and it's easy to serve with anything. I love to serve it with baked potatoes or egg noodles—you can even make sandwiches with it to keep things extra simple.

Traditionally, this recipe is made with a packet of ranch dressing mix, but I opted for a homemade version. All the spices I've included in this recipe will give the same flavor as a packet of ranch dressing mix but without having to keep one on hand.

Yield: **4–6 SERVINGS**

1 tbsp (15 ml) olive oil

3–4 lb (1.4–1.8 kg) beef chuck roast

1 tsp salt

½ tsp pepper

1½ cups (360 ml) beef broth

1 cup (120 g) pickled pepperoncini, whole or sliced

½ cup (60 g) sliced onion

1 tsp onion powder

½ tsp garlic powder

1 tsp parsley, dried

½ tsp basil, dried

½ tsp dill, dried

Heat the olive oil in a nonstick skillet over high heat. Season the beef roast with the salt and pepper. Sear the beef in the skillet for about 3 minutes per side. Place the seared beef, beef broth, pepperoncini, onion, onion powder, garlic powder, parsley, basil and dill in the slow cooker.

Cook on high for 4 hours or low for 8 hours. Shred and serve.

BBQ BEEF BRISKET

Everyone loves beef brisket, but everyone *really* loves this BBQ-sauced beef brisket! The homemade BBQ sauce is easy to make and totally worth the extra effort. I like the layered flavors of the spice mix on the meat with the sauce over the top. It really lets the BBQ flavors cook into the meat and makes every bite BBQ-flavored. We serve this on sandwiches, alongside coleslaw or even just with potatoes! It's super versatile, perfect for a crowd and a favorite of everyone who tries it.

Yield: **6–8 SERVINGS**

FOR THE BBQ SAUCE
½ cup (80 g) diced yellow onion

2 cloves garlic, minced

½ tsp dried mustard

⅛ tsp cayenne pepper

½ tsp salt

½ tsp pepper

I tsp prepared mustard

2 cups (480 ml) ketchup

2 tbsp (30 ml) molasses

2 tbsp (28 g) brown sugar

FOR THE SPICE MIX
2 tbsp (16 g) chili powder

I tbsp (7 g) paprika

I tsp salt

I tsp pepper

¼ tsp cayenne pepper, or to taste

⅛ tsp cloves

FOR THE BRISKET
I cup (240 ml) water

5 lb (2.3 kg) beef brisket (see Note)

Pickles, for serving, optional

To make the BBQ sauce, in a bowl, combine the onion, garlic, dried mustard, cayenne pepper, salt, pepper, prepared mustard, ketchup, molasses and brown sugar. Set aside.

To make the spice mix, in a separate bowl, combine the chili powder, paprika, salt, pepper, cayenne pepper and cloves. Set aside.

Place the water in the slow cooker. Rub the brisket with the spice mix. Place the brisket in the slow cooker. Pour the BBQ sauce over the top of the brisket.

Cook on high for 4 hours or low for 8 hours. When the brisket is finished cooking, shred and serve with pickles, if desired.

Note: Often when you purchase brisket, it is a very large cut. I usually trim mine down into 5-lb (2.3-kg) pieces so they are easier to cook and fit in a slow cooker.

THE EASIEST EVER BEEF BRISKET

Slow cooker beef brisket is cooked low and slow until it falls apart easily and all the fat is broken down. Layers of deep flavors cook into the brisket, making every bite delicious and tender. This inexpensive cut of beef is perfect for a crowd and is easy to prepare in a slow cooker.

I love to serve this over mashed potatoes or on thick slices of crusty bread. The sauce left in the slow cooker after the brisket is done cooking is delicious to serve on the side.

Yield: **6–8 SERVINGS**

2 cups (480 ml) beef broth

¾ cup (180 ml) soy sauce

¼ cup (60 ml) Worcestershire sauce

5 lb (2.3 kg) beef brisket (see Note)

½ tsp salt

½ tsp pepper

1 sprig fresh rosemary

8 fresh sage leaves

3 sprigs fresh thyme, plus 1 tsp fresh thyme, chopped, for garnish

1 tsp fresh parsley, chopped, for garnish

Combine the beef broth, soy sauce and Worcestershire sauce in the base of a large slow cooker. Place the brisket in the liquid, fat side up. Sprinkle the salt and pepper over the top of the brisket. Nestle the fresh rosemary, sage leaves and sprigs of thyme around the brisket.

Cook on low for 8 hours, or until the brisket is fork tender. I actually like to shred the brisket and let it sit in the sauce for a few minutes to soak up the deliciousness. Garnish with the fresh thyme and parsley before serving.

Note: Often when you purchase brisket, it is a very large cut. I usually trim mine down into 5-lb (2.3-kg) pieces so they are easier to cook and fit in a slow cooker.

HERBY BEEF STROGANOFF FROM SCRATCH

Herby beef stroganoff is traditionally a recipe that is made on the stovetop, but I love making it in the slow cooker. Often when you make beef stroganoff on the stovetop, you have to use a more expensive cut of meat, so it is tender enough with the short stovetop cooking time. By making this recipe in the slow cooker, you are able to use a less expensive cut of meat, like stew meat, and still have it turn out tender, flavorful and perfect every time.

Yield: **6 SERVINGS**

1 cup (160 g) chopped yellow onion

1 cup (70 g) sliced white mushrooms

4 cloves garlic, minced

2 sprigs sage

1 sprig thyme

½ tsp salt

¼ tsp pepper

2 tbsp (16 g) cornstarch

2 tbsp (30 ml) Worcestershire sauce

1 tsp soy sauce

1½ cups (360 ml) beef broth

1 lb (454 g) beef stew meat

2 tbsp (30 ml) heavy cream

⅓ cup (80 ml) sour cream

2 tbsp (8 g) fresh parsley, minced

1 lb (454 g) cooked pasta, for serving

Add the onion, mushrooms, garlic, sage, thyme, salt and pepper to the slow cooker. In a small bowl, whisk together the cornstarch, Worcestershire sauce and soy sauce. Add the mixture to the slow cooker. Add the beef broth and stew meat to the slow cooker and stir until combined.

Cook on high for 3 hours or low for 6 hours.

Add the heavy cream, sour cream and fresh parsley to the slow cooker. Stir until combined and cook for an additional 15 to 30 minutes on low heat. Serve over egg noodles.

ITALIAN BRAISED SHORT RIBS WITH VEGETABLES

In my opinion, short ribs are one of the most underused cuts of meat! They are perfect for slow cooking because they get nice and tender and start to fall off of the bone by the time they are done. Because they are small, they are also able to take on the other flavors in the recipe, so the entire short rib is packed with flavor.

I love the combination of flavors in this recipe. They are deep and rich, which is why adding the fresh herbs at the end is important. The fresh herbs cut through the richness and really brighten up the dish. The vegetables also add delicious variety to the flavor of this recipe. They pair well with the tender and flavorful meat and complete the recipe nicely.

Yield: **6 SERVINGS**

8 beef short ribs

1 tsp salt

½ tsp pepper

1 tbsp (15 ml) olive oil

6 oz (170 g) tomato paste

2 tbsp (30 ml) balsamic vinegar

1 cup (240 ml) beef broth

1 cup (240 ml) red wine (or additional beef broth)

2 carrots, diced

2 stalks celery, diced

1 medium yellow onion, diced

3 cloves garlic, minced

2 bay leaves

2 tsp (3 g) dried thyme

1 tsp dried oregano

2 tbsp (8 g) fresh parsley, minced, for garnish

2 tbsp (3 g) basil, fresh, minced, for garnish

Season the short ribs with the salt and pepper. Heat the olive oil in a medium skillet on high heat until the oil is smoking. Sear each side of the short ribs for about 3 minutes per side. Remove the ribs and set aside.

In a bowl, whisk together the tomato paste, balsamic vinegar, beef broth and red wine. Set aside.

Add the carrots, celery, onion, garlic, bay leaves, thyme and oregano to the slow cooker. Place the short ribs on top of the vegetables. Pour the liquid mixture over the top of the ribs and vegetables.

Cook on high for 4 hours or low for 8 hours. Garnish with the parsley and basil.

GARLIC AND THYME BEEF TIPS

This recipe is so simple but so satisfying. We love to serve this with potatoes or egg noodles. You will be surprised how easy it is to prepare: A little bit of measuring and whisking, and you have a great dinner ready to go in no time!

I like using beef stew meat in this recipe, because I often have it in my freezer. If you don't have stew meat, you can use almost any cut of meat that has been sliced into small pieces. It's a great recipe for using up tougher cuts of meat, because the long cooking time really makes it tender.

Yield: **6 SERVINGS**

1 cup (160 g) chopped yellow onion

4 cloves garlic, minced

2 sprigs sage

1 sprig thyme

½ tsp salt

¼ tsp pepper

2 tbsp (16 g) cornstarch

2 tbsp (30 ml) Worcestershire sauce

1 tsp soy sauce

1½ cups (360 ml) beef broth

1 lb (454 g) beef stew meat

Roasted potatoes, for serving, optional

Add the onion, garlic, sage, thyme, salt and pepper to the slow cooker. In a small bowl, whisk together the cornstarch, Worcestershire sauce, soy sauce and beef broth. Add the mixture to the slow cooker with the beef stew meat.

Cook on high for 4 hours or low for 8 hours.

Serve with roasted potatoes, if desired.

EASY BEEF BOURGUIGNON

Making beef bourguignon can often seem complicated and intimidating. This recipe takes away all of that stress and gives you the same amazing flavors with minimal effort. The hardest part of making this recipe is keeping your family from eating all the bacon you have fried while you are tossing everything else together in the slow cooker!

I like to use a chuck roast or a round roast for this recipe. Either one will work great, but I find that chuck roasts are usually easier to cube and brown evenly because of how they are cut.

Yield: **6 SERVINGS**

6 strips of bacon, chopped

3–4 lb (1.4–1.8 kg) beef roast, any kind, cut into 3-inch (8-cm) cubes

1 tsp salt

½ tsp pepper

3 cups (720 ml) red wine

4 medium potatoes, diced

3 carrots, chopped

8 oz (227 g) baby bella mushrooms, halved

1 medium yellow onion, diced

2 cups (480 ml) beef broth

2 beef bouillon cubes

2 bay leaves

2 sprigs thyme

3 tbsp (24 g) cornstarch

2 tbsp (8 g) fresh parsley, minced, for garnish

Place the chopped bacon in a cold skillet, then heat it on medium-low heat so the fat can render out slowly. Cook until the bacon is crispy, about 4 minutes. Remove the bacon from the skillet and set it aside, leaving the bacon grease in the pan. Season the cubed beef roast with the salt and pepper. In the same skillet, brown the meat in batches of three or four pieces at a time in the bacon grease, 3 to 5 minutes per side. Set the browned meat aside.

Add the red wine, potatoes, carrots, mushrooms, onion, beef broth, bouillon cubes, bay leaves, thyme and cornstarch to the slow cooker and stir thoroughly so that the cornstarch is combined. Nestle the bacon and the beef into the contents of the slow cooker.

Cook on high for 4 hours or low for 8 hours. Garnish with the fresh parsley.

THE BEST SALISBURY STEAK AND GRAVY

Salisbury steak and gravy is a classic meal that is so easy to make in the slow cooker. Often Salisbury steak can be tough and lack flavor. Making it in the slow cooker ensures that the steaks won't be dry. This recipe is great because it uses simple ingredients, but the flavors are intense and delicious! It pairs really well with a milder side dish because it's so savory.

Yield: **6 SERVINGS**

FOR THE STEAKS
3 tbsp (45 ml) milk

1 slice sandwich bread

1 lb (454 g) ground beef

2 tbsp (20 g) grated yellow onion

1 clove garlic, grated

2 tsp (10 ml) Worcestershire sauce

1 tbsp (17 g) tomato paste

1 egg

1 tsp salt

½ tsp pepper

1 tsp dried oregano

2 tsp (3 g) dried basil

2 tbsp (30 ml) olive oil

FOR THE GRAVY
½ medium yellow onion, sliced

8 oz (227 g) mushrooms, sliced

2 cups (480 ml) beef broth

2 tbsp (16 g) cornstarch

2 tbsp (33 g) tomato paste

2 tsp (10 ml) Worcestershire sauce

2 tbsp (8 g) fresh parsley, chopped, for garnish

4 cups (840 g) mashed potatoes, for serving

To make the steaks, pour the milk over the slice of bread in a shallow bowl and allow the bread to soak up all of the milk. Add the ground beef, grated onion, grated garlic, Worcestershire sauce, tomato paste, egg, salt, pepper, oregano and basil and stir together well. Form the steak mixture into six oval-shaped patties. Heat the olive oil on high heat in a nonstick skillet. Brown the steaks on each side, two or three at a time, about 3 minutes per side.

To make the gravy, combine the onion, mushrooms, beef broth, cornstarch, tomato paste and Worcestershire sauce in the slow cooker. Stir together well, then add the browned steaks to the slow cooker.

Cook on high for 4 hours or low for 8 hours. Garnish with the fresh parsley and serve with mashed potatoes.

GARLIC-BUTTER STEAK AND POTATOES

I wanted to find a way to make steak in a slow cooker that would satisfy everyone's differing opinions on what temperature the perfect steak should be cooked to. This slow cooker recipe gives you an easy way to make sure everyone gets the steak they want!

I really like the combination of steak and potatoes with the strong flavors in the butter. If you have time while the recipe is slow cooking, baste the steak and potatoes with the butter and broth mixture to make them extra succulent.

Yield: **6 SERVINGS**

2 lb (907 g) baby or fingerling potatoes

1 tsp salt

½ tsp red pepper flakes

1 cup (240 ml) beef broth

3 sprigs rosemary

2 tbsp (30 ml) olive oil

4 (6–8-oz [170–227-g]) rib-eye steaks (see Note)

4 tbsp (56 g) butter

4 cloves garlic, minced

Place the potatoes in the bottom of the slow cooker and add the salt and red pepper flakes. Pour in the beef broth and nestle the rosemary into the broth.

Cook on high for 3 hours or low for 6 hours.

While the potatoes are cooking, heat the olive oil in a skillet over high heat. Sear both sides of the steaks until they are golden brown, about 3 minutes per side. Remove them and set aside on a plate.

When the potatoes have finished the first cook time, place the steaks on top of the potatoes and pour in any accumulated juices from the plate. Place 1 tablespoon (14 g) of butter and one quarter of the garlic over the top of each steak. Leave the slow cooker heat on high and cook the potatoes and steaks for 1 hour for well-done (internal temperature of 165°F [75°C]), 30 minutes for medium (internal temperature of 155°F [70°C]) or 15 minutes for medium-rare (internal temperature of 140°F [60°C]).

Note: You can use any kind of steak you have or prefer. I like the way the rib-eye steaks fit into the slow cooker, but this is up to your discretion.

ONION AND THYME FRENCH DIP SANDWICHES

Onion and thyme French dip sandwiches are practically exploding with flavor. They are one of my husband's favorite meals. I love making these when I know he has a particularly long day ahead of him. The meat stays warm in the slow cooker, and then broiling the sandwiches only takes a few minutes when everyone is finally home together.

Yield: **6–8 SERVINGS**

2 tbsp (30 ml) olive oil

2–3 lb (908 g–1.4 kg) beef chuck roast

1 tsp salt

½ tsp pepper

4 medium yellow onions, sliced

1 cup (240 ml) beef broth

3 tbsp (45 ml) Worcestershire sauce

1 tbsp (15 ml) soy sauce

6 sprigs thyme, plus 2 tsp (1 g), for garnish

6 crusty rolls

3 tbsp (42 g) butter, softened

12 slices provolone or Swiss cheese

In a large nonstick skillet, heat the olive oil over high heat. Season the roast with the salt and pepper, rubbing it into the meat. Sear both sides of the roast in the skillet, about 3 minutes per side. Set aside the browned meat when finished. Place the sliced onions in the bottom of the slow cooker. Place the browned roast on top of the sliced onions. Pour the beef broth, Worcestershire sauce and soy sauce over the roast. Place the thyme in the slow cooker.

Cook the beef roast and onions on high for 4 hours or low for 8 hours.

Remove the cooked beef and shred it with two forks. Place the shredded beef back in the slow cooker with the onions. Allow the shredded beef to rest in the slow cooker for 30 minutes on high.

Slice the crusty rolls in half, as for sandwiches. Spread the butter evenly over the rolls. Heat a nonstick skillet over medium heat and toast the rolls until golden brown.

For melted cheese on the sandwiches, preheat the oven to 350°F (175°C). Build the French dip sandwiches by piling the beef and onion mixture over the rolls and topping with slices of cheese. If desired, wrap the sandwiches in foil and heat them in the oven until the cheese is melted, about 10 minutes.

Strain the remaining liquid in the slow cooker and serve on the side with the sandwiches for dipping. Garnish with additional fresh thyme.

SAVORY BEEF POT PIE

While most people think of pot pie as containing chicken, this beef version is packed with all the comforting goodness you want in a pot pie, but with extra flavor. This recipe is rich and filling. It's perfect for a dinner after a cold day working outside or a long day at the office. The biscuit topping is soft and tender but also flaky, as a biscuit should be.

Yield: **6 SERVINGS**

FOR THE FILLING
1 lb (454 g) ground beef

½ cup (80 g) diced yellow onion

½ cup (65 g) diced carrots

1 cup (150 g) peeled and diced gold or red potatoes

3 tbsp (24 g) flour

1 (15-oz [425-g]) can diced tomatoes

2 cups (480 ml) beef broth

2 tsp (10 ml) Worcestershire sauce

1 tsp soy sauce

1 tsp dried oregano

½ tsp salt

¼ tsp pepper

½ cup (65 g) frozen peas

FOR THE BISCUIT TOPPING
1¾ cups (220 g) all-purpose flour, divided

3 tsp (14 g) baking powder

¾ tsp salt

4 tbsp (56 g) butter

¾ cup (180 ml) cold milk

2 tsp (3 g) fresh parsley, minced, for garnish

To make the filling, in a dry medium skillet over medium heat, cook the ground beef until it is browned, 5 to 7 minutes. Combine the browned ground beef, onion, carrots, potatoes and flour in the slow cooker. Add the can of tomatoes, beef broth, Worcestershire sauce and soy sauce to the slow cooker and stir until everything is well combined. Add the oregano, salt and pepper and stir again until the ingredients are combined.

Cook on high for 2 hours or low for 6 hours. Add the peas and stir to combine.

To make the biscuit topping, while the filling is cooking, in a large bowl combine 1½ cups (190 g) of the flour, the baking powder and the salt. In a small dish, melt the butter, then immediately add the melted butter to the cold milk. Stir until the butter starts to solidify again and small shards of butter are visible. Add the butter and milk to the dry ingredients, adding more flour if it is needed. The dough should be evenly moist but easily handled and not sticky. Working with a few tablespoons of dough at a time, roll gently into a ball and flatten with your hand. Gently set each flattened ball on top of the pot pie filling in the slow cooker. Repeat until the top is covered and you have used up all the dough. Cook for 1 to 2 more hours on low (or 30 minutes to 1 hour on high), until the biscuit dough is cooked through. The biscuits may look slightly moist on top but should be cooked through when pulled apart.

If you would like, place the insert of the slow cooker in the oven and broil on high for about 3 minutes to get a nice brown on top. Sprinkle with the fresh parsley.

SIMPLE ROSEMARY AND OREGANO BRAISED BEEF

Braised beef is a simple recipe but one of my favorites! Searing the beef in multiple pieces before slow cooking it creates delicious crispy edges on the meat. Those are my favorite part!

This is great served with anything, truly. We like to pair it with cheesy potatoes or mashed potatoes. My other favorite thing about this recipe is all the possibilities for the leftovers . . . if you have any! Leftover braised beef makes amazing tacos and enchiladas.

Yield: **4–6 SERVINGS**

1 tbsp (15 ml) olive oil

3–4 lb (1.4–1.8 kg) chuck roast, cut into 4 to 6 pieces

1 tsp salt

½ tsp pepper

1½ cups (360 ml) beef broth

3 rosemary sprigs, plus ½ tsp, for garnish

2 oregano sprigs, plus ½ tsp, for garnish

Heat the olive oil in a nonstick skillet over high heat. Season the beef pieces with the salt and pepper. Sear the beef in the skillet, about 3 minutes per side. Don't crowd the pan. You want the pieces to get a nice golden-brown crust quickly, because most of the cooking will happen in the slow cooker.

Place the seared beef in the slow cooker. Add the beef broth, rosemary sprigs and oregano sprigs.

Cook on high for 3 hours or low for 6 hours. Garnish with the additional rosemary and oregano.

CORNED BEEF AND CABBAGE

Corned beef and cabbage is another classic dish that is made *so* easily in the slow cooker. It's so easy that you can put it together in less than 5 minutes!

Corned beef is brisket that has been salt-cured. It is not cooked when you purchase it, just cured so that it becomes extra tender as it cooks. Be sure that you always cut the corned beef across the grain; this ensures it will be nice and tender when it is served.

Yield: **6 SERVINGS**

4 potatoes, diced

2 carrots, chopped

½ head cabbage, cut into 2-inch (5-cm) wedges

1 tsp salt

½ tsp pepper

2 cups (480 ml) beef broth

2 bay leaves

3–4 lb (1.4–1.8 kg) corned beef brisket, with seasoning pack

2 tbsp (8 g) fresh parsley, minced, for garnish

Place the potatoes, carrots, cabbage, salt, pepper, beef broth and bay leaves in the slow cooker. Place the corned beef on top of the vegetables. Sprinkle the seasoning pack contents over the top of the brisket.

Cook on high for 4 hours or low for 8 hours. Garnish with the fresh parsley.

SUPER SIMPLE BARBACOA BEEF

Barbacoa beef is a delicious spicy and smoky beef recipe that our family loves. It is just as good as anything you could purchase in a restaurant—maybe even better! Each bite is a surprise of complex flavors, but even with all the flavors, it does not feel too heavy.

We eat this in tacos, over rice or in quesadillas. Any way you serve it, there won't be anything left! The fresh cilantro at the end really brightens up all the flavors and brings out the smoky flavors in the beef.

Yield: **4–6 SERVINGS**

1 tbsp (15 ml) olive oil

3–4 lb (1.4–1.8 kg) chuck roast, cut into 4 to 6 pieces

1 tsp salt

½ tsp pepper

1½ cups (360 ml) beef broth

4 chilies in adobo

1½ tbsp (9 g) cumin

4 cloves garlic, minced

¼ cup (60 ml) lime juice

3 bay leaves

2 sprigs fresh oregano

¼ tsp cloves

¼ cup (4 g) fresh cilantro, chopped

Heat the olive oil in a nonstick skillet over high heat. Season the beef pieces with the salt and pepper. Sear the beef in the skillet, about 3 minutes per side. Don't crowd the pan. You want the pieces to get a nice golden-brown crust quickly, because most of the cooking will happen in the slow cooker.

Place the seared beef, beef broth, chilies, cumin, garlic, lime juice, bay leaves, oregano and cloves in the slow cooker.

Cook on high for 4 hours or low for 8 hours. Shred the beef and stir in the chopped cilantro.

SAVORY POULTRY RECIPES

Chicken is a staple in every home kitchen, but sometimes it's easy to get stuck in a chicken recipe rut! I specifically wrote each one of these recipes to be flavorful and fresh and to shine a new light on preparing chicken in the slow cooker.

One of the easiest ways to set yourself up for success when cooking chicken breasts in the slow cooker is to choose cuts of chicken that are medium sized. Large chicken breasts can still taste dry even if they've been slow cooked. Medium sized is the way to go. It allows the meat to cook until it's tender and absorb the flavors of the dish without overcooking.

These recipes are no-fuss favorites. My family particularly loves the Sage and Butter Braised Whole Chicken (page 42), Thyme and Garlic Chicken Marsala (page 61) and Simple Salsa Verde Chicken (page 66). These dishes are guaranteed to be a hit with even the pickiest of eaters in your family. They are filled with familiar ingredients, but the end results are anything but basic. My kids' number one dinner requests come from these savory poultry recipes, and I'm always happy to oblige! Although they are perfect for kids, adults will love them too.

SAGE AND BUTTER BRAISED WHOLE CHICKEN

If you need a simple but delicious way to prepare a whole chicken, this is the perfect recipe. The sage and butter create an amazing flavor that really cooks into the chicken while it is in the slow cooker. This recipe comes out perfect every single time and eliminates any guesswork about if the chicken is done, it if will be dry or if everyone will love it! I guarantee they will.

Yield: **4–6 SERVINGS**

2 medium yellow onions, quartered

2 cloves garlic, crushed

4 tbsp (56 g) butter, cubed

3 sprigs sage

1 sprig thyme

1 cup (240 ml) chicken broth

1 (3–5-lb [1.4–2.3-kg]) whole chicken

2 tsp (12 g) salt

1 tsp pepper

Place the onions, garlic, butter, sage, thyme and chicken broth in the slow cooker. Place the whole chicken on top and season the chicken with salt and pepper.

Cook on high for 4 hours or low for 8 hours. If possible, baste the chicken with the liquid in the bottom of the slow cooker every few hours. If you would like crisp skin on the chicken, place it on a sheet tray after it is done cooking in the slow cooker and broil it for about 5 minutes, until it is lightly golden brown.

CREAMY SUN-DRIED TOMATO CHICKEN

This delicious dish has bold Italian flavors. Sun-dried tomatoes pair so well with the creamy sauce and flavors from the fresh herbs. One of the reasons I love this recipe is because it speaks to my Italian heritage. I actually developed this recipe because I had homemade sun-dried tomatoes from my mother that I needed to use and, because the Italian in our family comes from her side, I thought it would be the perfect tribute to that heritage!

Yield: **4–6 SERVINGS**

1½ cups (360 ml) chicken broth

4 oz (114 g) oil-packed sun-dried tomatoes, drained and minced

½ tsp salt

¼ tsp pepper

1 clove garlic, minced

4 chicken breasts, boneless and skinless, halved lengthwise

1 cup (240 ml) heavy cream

1 cup (25 g) fresh spinach, chopped or whole

¼ cup plus 2 tbsp (30 g) Parmesan cheese, shredded, divided

2 tbsp (3 g) fresh basil, chopped, for garnish

1 tbsp (4 g) fresh parsley, chopped, for garnish

1 lb (454 g) cooked pasta, for serving (I prefer fettuccine)

In the slow cooker, combine the broth, tomatoes, salt, pepper and garlic. Nestle the chicken breasts into the mixture. Turn the slow cooker on high for 2 hours or low for 4 hours.

Add the heavy cream, spinach and ¼ cup (20 g) Parmesan cheese and replace the lid. Let it cook for about 30 minutes on low, or until the spinach is wilted and the cheese is melted through. Garnish with the remaining 2 tablespoons (10 g) Parmesan cheese, basil and parsley and serve with the pasta.

LEMONY BASIL CHICKEN

This recipe is so simple yet packed with flavor. I love the combination of lemon and basil; it's so refreshing and light! Searing the chicken before slow cooking it gives it an added layer of flavor that really enhances the other elements of the dish.

I recommend serving this with pasta or rice, or any mild-tasting side dish. If you want to go extra light, simply add a quick veggie like peas or roasted carrots.

Yield: **4–6 SERVINGS**

1 tbsp (15 ml) olive oil

6 medium chicken breasts, boneless and skinless

2 tsp (3 g) dried basil

1 tsp salt

½ tsp pepper

1½ cups (360 ml) chicken broth

½ cup (120 ml) fresh-squeezed lemon juice

¼ cup (6 g) fresh basil, for garnish

2 lemons, cut into wedges, for garnish

Heat the olive oil in a nonstick skillet over high heat. Sprinkle the chicken breasts with the dried basil, salt and pepper. Sear the chicken breasts, two or three at a time, in the skillet, about 3 minutes per side. Don't crowd the pan, because you want them to get a nice golden-brown crust quickly; most of the cooking will happen in the slow cooker.

Place the seared chicken breasts in the slow cooker. Add the chicken broth and lemon juice to the slow cooker.

Cook on low for 6 hours or high for 4 hours.

Stack the basil leaves on top of each other and then roll the stack into a cylinder. Slice across the cylinder to create long, thin strands of basil. When the chicken is done cooking, garnish with the fresh basil and lemon wedges.

THYME-BRAISED CHICKEN BREASTS

This recipe is one of my favorites because it is a version of a dinner my dad used to cook when I was a kid. He would make braised chicken breasts and scalloped potatoes on Sundays for family dinner, and I knew I wanted to honor that memory by re-creating his recipe in this book.

This dish is simple but tasty. The thyme infuses the broth and chicken and creates a really deep flavor throughout the dish. I know it will help create many special moments around the dinner table at your home, too.

Yield: **4–6 SERVINGS**

1 tbsp (15 ml) olive oil

6 medium chicken breasts, boneless and skinless

1 tsp salt

½ tsp pepper

2 cloves garlic, minced

1½ cups (360 ml) chicken broth

3 sprigs fresh thyme, plus more for garnish

Heat the olive oil in a nonstick skillet over high heat. Season the chicken breasts with the salt and pepper. Sear the chicken breasts, two or three at a time, in the skillet, about 3 minutes per side. Don't crowd the pan, because you want the chicken breasts to get a nice golden-brown crust quickly; most of the cooking will happen in the slow cooker.

Place the seared chicken breasts in the slow cooker. Add the garlic, chicken broth and thyme.

Cook on low for 6 hours or high for 3 hours. Garnish with more fresh thyme.

CREAMY MUSHROOM CHICKEN

Creamy mushroom chicken is a delicious homemade version of an old favorite. My kids are crazy about mushrooms and can't get enough of this recipe. When you add the mushrooms, it will seem like a lot, but they cook down significantly and add to the liquid in the slow cooker. This dish ends up perfectly creamy, with lots of mushroom, sage and thyme flavors.

Yield: **4–6 SERVINGS**

1 tsp salt

½ tsp pepper

½ tsp ground sage

1 clove garlic, minced

1 cup (240 ml) chicken broth

1 lb (454 g) baby bella mushrooms, sliced

4 medium chicken breasts, boneless and skinless

1 sprig thyme, plus more for garnish

½ cup (120 ml) heavy cream

1 tbsp (4 g) fresh parsley, minced

Combine the salt, pepper, sage, garlic and chicken broth in the slow cooker. Add the mushrooms to the slow cooker. Place the chicken breasts on top of the mushrooms, and add the sprig of thyme on top.

Cook on high for 3 hours or low for 6 hours. Add the heavy cream and minced parsley to the slow cooker. Replace the lid and cook on low for 30 minutes, or until the cream is warmed through. Garnish with additional thyme.

GARLIC AND SAGE TURKEY BREAST WITH GREEN BEANS

I love cooking turkey and not just at Thanksgiving! While this would make an excellent holiday meal, it is also perfect for any day of the week. When I have a stock of turkey in my freezer, this recipe is a quick way to make a delicious dinner.

The first time I made this recipe, my family was very skeptical. They thought that the only good turkey was one that came out of the oven! They were happily mistaken, though, and this recipe quickly became an often-requested favorite.

Yield: **4–6 SERVINGS**

1 medium yellow
onion, quartered

6 cloves garlic, crushed

3 sprigs sage

1 sprig rosemary

1 cup (240 ml) chicken broth

1 tbsp (15 ml) honey

1 (10-lb [4.5-kg]) skin-on
turkey breast

2 tsp (12 g) salt

1 tsp pepper

12 oz (340 g) fresh green
beans, trimmed

Place the onion, garlic, sage, rosemary, chicken broth and honey in the slow cooker. Season the turkey breast with the salt and pepper. Place the turkey breast in the slow cooker, nestling it into the liquid.

Cook on high for 3 hours or low for 7 hours. If possible, baste the turkey with the liquid in the bottom of the slow cooker every few hours. Add the green beans for the last hour of the cooking time, nestling them down around the turkey breast. If you would like crisp skin on the turkey, place it on a sheet tray after it is done cooking and broil it for about 5 minutes, until it is lightly golden brown.

GREEK CHICKEN DINNER

This dish is packed with bold flavors and lots of color. I love Greek flavors, but it took a few tries to find the right balance and keep them from overpowering each other or the chicken. I settled on adding some of the ingredients *after* cooking to solve that problem. It allows the chicken to take on the milder flavors of the oregano, onion and garlic while cooking but still get that punch of fresh tang from lemons and salty olives and feta you expect from Greek recipes.

Yield: **4–6 SERVINGS**

¼ cup (60 ml) olive oil

4 cloves garlic, minced

1 tsp dried basil

1 tsp salt

¼ tsp pepper

1 cup (240 ml) chicken broth

1½ lb (680 g) whole baby potatoes, red or gold

1 cup (160 g) chopped red onion

6 chicken thighs, boneless and skinless

3 sprigs oregano, divided

1 cup (135 g) jarred Kalamata olives, pitted

1 lemon, juiced

8 oz (227 g) crumbled goat cheese or feta cheese

⅓ cup (20 g) fresh parsley, minced

In a small bowl, combine the olive oil, garlic, basil, salt and pepper. Set aside. Pour the chicken broth into the slow cooker. Place the baby potatoes and the onion into the broth. Place the chicken thighs on top of the potatoes and the onion. Pour the olive oil mixture over the top of the chicken thighs. Add two sprigs of oregano to the slow cooker.

Cook on high for 3 hours or low for 6 hours. Garnish with the remaining oregano, and add the Kalamata olives, lemon juice, cheese and fresh parsley.

DUMP-AND-GO HONEY GARLIC CHICKEN AND GREEN BEANS

On our farm, we raise bees along with our other animals. This means we always have a delicious stock of honey just waiting to be used in recipes like this one! The flavors in this dish are perfectly opposite, spicy and sweet, which makes it taste amazing.

I love adding the frozen green beans at the very end—it simplifies dinner that much more, and they are easy to keep on hand. Who doesn't appreciate an easy meal that already includes a veggie?

Yield: **4–6 SERVINGS**

½ tsp salt

¼ tsp red pepper flakes

5 cloves garlic, minced

½ cup (120 ml) honey

1 tbsp (15 ml) soy sauce

3 tbsp (24 g) cornstarch

1½ cups (360 ml) chicken broth

5–6 boneless, skinless chicken breasts

3 sprigs thyme

2 cups (242 g) frozen green beans

Whisk together the salt, red pepper flakes, garlic, honey, soy sauce, cornstarch and chicken broth in the slow cooker. Place the chicken breasts in the liquid mixture in the slow cooker. Add the thyme on top of the chicken.

Cook on high for 3 hours or low for 7 hours. Add the green beans to the slow cooker on top of the chicken. Cook for an additional 30 minutes on high or 1 hour on low.

NO-PREP HONEY MUSTARD CHICKEN

Mustard is one of my favorite flavors to pair with chicken. I love the tang it brings to the dish and the sweet aftertaste from the honey. Sage complements chicken, but it goes especially well with mustard. The prep for this recipe is great, too—there is none!

Yield: **4–6 SERVINGS**

½ tsp salt

¼ tsp pepper

1 clove garlic, minced

½ cup (120 ml) stone-ground mustard

½ cup (120 ml) honey

1½ cups (360 ml) chicken broth

5–6 chicken breasts, boneless and skinless

3 sprigs sage

Whisk together the salt, pepper, garlic, mustard, honey and chicken broth in the slow cooker. Place the chicken breasts in the liquid mixture in the slow cooker. Add the sage on top of the chicken.

Cook on high for 4 hours or low for 8 hours.

THYME AND GARLIC CHICKEN MARSALA

Chicken Marsala is a classic dish loved by many. This recipe starts out like most chicken Marsala recipes, but, of course, it's finished out in a slow cooker, which allows all of the flavors—chicken, shallot, wine and garlic—to meld. The slow cooker also gives the mushrooms a chance to cook down and really take on the flavors in the sauce. This is delicious over pasta.

Yield: **4–6 SERVINGS**

1 tbsp (15 ml) olive oil

3 chicken breasts, boneless and skinless

1 tsp salt

½ tsp pepper

½ cup (65 g) flour

1 shallot, minced

2 cloves garlic, minced

1 cup (240 ml) chicken broth

⅔ cup (160 ml) Marsala wine

8 oz (227 g) baby bella mushrooms, sliced

3 sprigs fresh thyme

⅔ cup (160 ml) heavy cream

2 tbsp (8 g) fresh parsley, minced, for garnish

Heat the olive oil in a nonstick skillet over high heat. Slice each chicken breast in half lengthwise so you are left with 6 thinner pieces of chicken. Season each piece of chicken on both sides with the salt and pepper. Dredge the chicken pieces in the flour. Sear the floured chicken breasts, two or three at a time, in the skillet, about 3 minutes per side. Don't crowd the pan, because you want them to get a nice golden-brown crust quickly; most of the cooking will happen in the slow cooker.

Add the shallot, garlic, chicken broth, wine and mushrooms to the slow cooker. Place the seared chicken breasts in the slow cooker and add the sprigs of thyme on top.

Cook on low for 6 hours or high for 3 hours. Stir in the heavy cream and cook for 30 minutes on low. Garnish with the fresh parsley.

CHICKEN AND RICE "BAKE"

This recipe is a great one-pan dinner! I love making everything in the same dish, and this recipe fits that bill. Even though everything is cooked together, it isn't mushy and turns out perfect every time. The chicken is tender, the rice is cooked through and everything is perfectly spiced.

I like to nestle the thyme and sage down in the slow cooker, because it really gives them a chance to flavor the cooking liquid and therefore the rice. I add the parsley at the end because it gives the dish a nice fresh punch to finish things off.

Yield: **4–6 SERVINGS**

1½ cups (275 g) white rice (see Note)

1½ cups (360 ml) water

1½ cups (360 ml) chicken broth

½ cup (80 g) minced yellow onion

2 cloves garlic, minced

6–8 chicken tenders

1 tsp salt

½ tsp pepper

½ tsp onion powder

½ tsp garlic powder

½ tsp paprika

1 tsp ground thyme, dried

½ tsp ground sage, dried

2 tbsp (8 g) fresh parsley, minced, for garnish

Combine the rice, water, chicken broth, onion and garlic in the slow cooker. Place the chicken tenders on top of the rice.

Combine the salt, pepper, onion powder, garlic powder, paprika, thyme and sage in a small bowl, then sprinkle the mixture over the top of the chicken and rice.

Cook on high for 3 hours or low for 6 hours, until the rice is cooked and the chicken is tender. Garnish with the fresh parsley.

Note: I use medium-grain white rice. Long-grain white rice can also be used in this recipe, but instant rice and brown rice won't cook as expected.

EASY CHICKEN FAJITAS

Chicken fajitas are one of my favorite meals. Making the chicken in the slow cooker is a great way to get a filling but fresh dinner without having to make it right before serving. I love how tender the chicken and veggies get as they cook. The fresh lime juice combined with the spices in this dish really pack a flavorful punch!

This is one of those recipes that keeps on giving, even after you eat it for dinner. We love eating the leftovers in quesadillas. Sometimes my kids even request that I make the fajitas into quesadillas right away!

Yield: **4–6 SERVINGS**

FOR THE FAJITAS
3 chicken breasts, sliced into bite-size pieces

1 red bell pepper, sliced

1 green bell pepper, sliced

1 yellow bell pepper, sliced

1 red onion, sliced

2 cloves garlic, minced

1 tbsp (8 g) chili powder

½ tbsp (3 g) cumin

1 tsp salt

¼ cup (60 ml) lime juice

1 cup (240 ml) chicken broth

FOR SERVING
Small tortillas

Fresh cilantro, chopped

Cheddar cheese, shredded

Sour cream

Combine the chicken breasts, bell peppers, onion, garlic, chili powder, cumin, salt, lime juice and chicken broth in the slow cooker. Stir gently until everything is coated in the spices.

Cook on high for 3 hours or low for 6 hours. Serve on tortillas with cilantro, Cheddar cheese, sour cream or any of your other favorite toppings.

SIMPLE SALSA VERDE CHICKEN

This recipe is so simple, but it is one of the most requested recipes at my house. We love the flavor combination of the chicken and salsa verde. Using homemade salsa verde makes this meal even more delicious!

Our favorite way to serve this recipe is in what we like to call "taco rice." We start with rice and layer on the salsa verde chicken along with crushed corn chips, lettuce, tomatoes, cheese and sour cream. It's delicious and so easy!

Yield: **4–6 SERVINGS**

FOR THE SALSA VERDE
1 lb (454 g) fresh tomatillos

2 medium jalapeño peppers

3 cloves garlic, skin on

1 medium yellow onion, quartered

1 tbsp (30 ml) lime juice

1 tsp salt

½ cup (8 g) fresh cilantro

FOR THE CHICKEN
2 cups (480 ml) salsa verde (see Note)

½ cup (120 ml) chicken broth

4 boneless, skinless chicken breasts

1 (15-oz [425-g]) can black beans

Preheat the oven to 425°F (220°C). Line a sheet tray with parchment paper, or grease it with oil or cooking spray.

To make the salsa verde, remove the husks from the tomatillos and place them on the prepared sheet tray along with the jalapeño peppers, garlic cloves and quartered onion. Roast the vegetables in the oven for 15 minutes, or until the skin starts to become bubbly and charred. Remove the tray from the oven and allow the vegetables to cool slightly. Remove the stem, skin and seeds from the jalapeños and the skin from the garlic cloves. Add the vegetables to a blender or food processor with the lime juice, salt and cilantro. Blend or process until mostly smooth, about 15 to 20 pulses. The consistency should be smooth, not chunky.

To make the chicken, whisk together the salsa verde and chicken broth in the slow cooker. Place the chicken in the slow cooker.

Cook on high for 4 hours or low for 8 hours. Shred the chicken and add the black beans. Stir until combined. Cook for an additional 30 minutes on high.

Note: You can also use store-bought salsa verde to keep things simple! For 2 cups (480 ml), use 1 (16-oz [484-g]) jar.

STUFFED PESTO CHICKEN

Stuffed pesto chicken is the perfect recipe to make when you need to impress someone but don't have a lot of time! Even though it's super easy to prepare, the flavors are amazing, and it looks complicated. Creating a pocket in the chicken for the pesto and cheese really allows all of the flavors to penetrate the chicken and make every bite extra flavorful.

Balsamic glaze is something you can buy in the store or make yourself. It is concentrated and slightly sweetened balsamic vinegar. If you decide to make it yourself, be sure to use a very high-quality balsamic vinegar, otherwise it can taste bitter. Whether store-bought or homemade, it adds a nice punch to this recipe and brightens up all of the other flavors. This pesto chicken goes well with pasta.

Yield: **4–6 SERVINGS**

FOR THE PESTO
2 cups (50 g) fresh basil leaves, packed into the cup

2 cloves garlic

¼ cup (30 g) pine nuts

⅓ cup (25 g) Parmesan cheese, shredded

1 tsp lemon juice

¼ tsp salt

⅓ cup (80 ml) olive oil or enough to bring pesto to desired consistency

FOR THE CHICKEN
4 skinless, boneless chicken breasts

1 cup (240 ml) chicken broth

1 cup (230 g) basil pesto

1 cup (112 g) mozzarella cheese, shredded

1 tsp salt

½ tsp pepper

1 pint (300 g) cherry tomatoes

¼ cup (60 ml) balsamic glaze, optional

2 tbsp (3 g) fresh basil, chopped, for garnish

FOR THE BALSAMIC GLAZE
2 cups (480 ml) high-quality balsamic vinegar

½ cup (110 g) brown sugar

To make the pesto, add the basil, garlic, pine nuts, Parmesan cheese, lemon juice and salt to a blender or food processor. Pulse until all of the ingredients are the same size and ground together, about ten pulses. Turn the food processor on and drizzle the olive oil in gradually, checking the consistency as you add the oil to the pesto. The pesto should be thick enough to easily stay on a spoon.

To make the chicken, slice a pocket into the side of each chicken breast. This is most easily done by acting as if you are going to slice each chicken breast in half lengthwise but stopping before you reach the back of the breast and thin end of the breast.

Pour the chicken broth into the bottom of the slow cooker. Place the sliced chicken breasts into the broth so that the sliced section is facing up. Divide the pesto evenly between all of the chicken breasts, spooning it into the pocket you created in each breast. Divide the mozzarella cheese evenly between all of the chicken breasts, filling each pocket. Sprinkle the salt and pepper over the top of each chicken breast. Pour the cherry tomatoes into the slow cooker.

Cook on high for 4 hours or low for 8 hours.

To make the balsamic glaze, if using, add the balsamic vinegar and brown sugar to a medium saucepan set over medium heat. Stir to combine and let the ingredients come to a boil, then reduce the heat to medium-low and let the mixture simmer until the balsamic glaze is thick and reduced by half, about 20 minutes, stirring occasionally. When it is ready it should coat the back of a spoon and leave a trail when you drag your finger through it. Let the glaze cool.

Drizzle each breast with the balsamic glaze, if desired, and top with the fresh basil.

*See image on page 40.

FLAVOR-PACKED PORK RECIPES

These are some of our family's favorite recipes. We always seem to prepare pork when we have family and friends over for a gathering. So of course these recipes taste delicious, but the flavors are also reminiscent of time spent with old friends and time making new ones. Whether it's a casual party or a holiday meal, these recipes will be a hit.

I love pairing bold flavors with pork, because it maintains its own distinct flavor while also taking on enough of the other flavors in the dish to create a tasty harmony between the ingredients. Cooking pork chops in the slow cooker allows them to stay really moist and make great individual portions. Thicker cut chops work best in the slow cooker, because the cooking time is long. Any cut will work as well; these recipes are easy and versatile.

Don't be scared by the flavor combinations in some of these recipes; I promise you won't be disappointed when you give them a try. Pork goes great with a little something sweet. The sweetness can balance the fatty flavor of the pork to create a lighter-tasting—but still filling—meal. I know you'll love every single recipe from this chapter.

PORK ROAST WITH FRESH APPLE SLAW

This pork roast has very subtle flavors, and pairing it with a fresh apple slaw really enhances them! The fresh apple slaw can be made up to 2 days ahead of time. The flavors continue to develop as it rests, and the lime juice keeps the apples fresh. We love serving this pork in a variety of ways, such as over egg noodles, in tacos or even on sandwiches.

Yield: **6–8 SERVINGS**

FOR THE PORK ROAST

2 tsp (12 g) salt

I tsp pepper

I tbsp (6 g) cumin

2 tbsp (16 g) chili powder

½ tbsp (3 g) ground coriander

2 tsp (5 g) paprika

3 cloves garlic, minced

2 medium yellow onions, halved

I cup (240 ml) apple juice

3–4 lb (1.4–1.8 kg) pork shoulder roast (also called a pork butt roast)

FOR THE APPLE SLAW

2 apples, any kind, sliced into matchsticks

½ head purple cabbage, sliced thin or shredded

⅓ cup (16 g) scallions, green and white section, sliced thin

½ cup (8 g) cilantro, chopped

⅓ cup (80 ml) lime juice

2 tbsp (30 ml) Dijon mustard

I tbsp (15 ml) honey

½ cup (120 ml) olive oil

½ tsp salt

Lime wedges, for serving

To make the pork roast, combine the salt, pepper, cumin, chili powder, coriander, paprika, garlic, onions and apple juice in the slow cooker. Add the pork roast and nestle it into the other ingredients.

Cook on high for 4 hours or low for 8 hours.

Meanwhile, make the apple slaw. In a large bowl, combine the apples, cabbage, scallions and cilantro. In a separate small bowl, whisk together the lime juice, Dijon mustard, honey, olive oil and salt. Pour the dressing mixture over the apple slaw and toss everything to combine. If you are making the apple slaw ahead of time, store it in the refrigerator for up to 2 days.

When the pork is done cooking, shred and serve with the apple slaw and lime wedges.

DUMP-AND-GO BBQ PULLED PORK

Dump-and-go recipes are some of my favorites. They are a snap to prep and then all you have to do is shred and serve! This pulled pork recipe is a staple in our house and is adored by everyone who tries it. We love eating it in sandwich form, but you can serve it any way you like.

I like adding extra spices and ingredients to the BBQ sauce to bolster the flavor and emphasize what is already in the sauce.

Yield: **6–8 SERVINGS**

2 tsp (12 g) salt

1 tsp pepper

3 cloves garlic, minced

2 medium yellow onions, halved

1 tbsp (7 g) paprika

¼ cup (55 g) brown sugar

2 cups (480 ml) BBQ sauce

½ cup (120 ml) water

3–4 lb (1.4–1.8 kg) pork shoulder roast (also called a pork butt roast)

½ cup (8 g) chopped cilantro

2 cups (140 g) cabbage, for serving

6–8 hamburger buns, for serving

Combine the salt, pepper, garlic, onions, paprika, brown sugar, BBQ sauce and water in the slow cooker. Add the pork roast and nestle it into the other ingredients.

Cook on high for 4 hours or low for 8 hours. When the pork is finished cooking, shred it and return it to the sauce. I recommend shredding the pork about 20 minutes before you want to serve it and letting it sit in the sauce to really absorb all of the flavors. Toss the pork with the cilantro before serving with cabbage on hamburger buns.

FARMHOUSE PORK CHOPS AND POTATOES

Creamy pork chops and potatoes is a delicious rib-sticking dinner that your whole family will love. Layers of potatoes and caramelized onions are topped with a creamy white sauce and browned pork chops.

Even if you or your family aren't big fans of onions, give this recipe a try! I have a family full of onion haters (I personally love them), and they still love this recipe. The onions add an amazing flavor you just can't get any other way. Trust me when I say this recipe will get rave reviews from everyone.

Yield: **6–8 SERVINGS**

2 tbsp (30 ml) olive oil

2 medium yellow onions, sliced

3 tbsp (42 g) butter

¼ cup (30 g) flour

I cup (240 ml) milk

I cup (240 ml) chicken broth

½ tsp dried sage

I tsp dried thyme, plus more for garnish

I tsp salt

½ tsp pepper

4 large potatoes, sliced

6 pork chops

Fresh parsley, for garnish

Add the olive oil to a large sauté pan. Sauté the onions over medium-low heat for 8 to 10 minutes or until softened and golden brown. Remove the onions from the pan and set aside. Melt the butter in the same pan. Add the flour and stir it until it is cooked and golden brown, about 2 minutes over medium-low heat. Add the milk and chicken broth and whisk until smooth and thickened, about 3 minutes. Add the sage, thyme, salt and pepper and whisk to combine. Layer the potatoes and onions in the slow cooker. Pour the sauce over the top of the potatoes and onions. Lay the pork chops evenly in one layer over the top of the potatoes.

Cook on high for 4 hours or low for 8 hours or until the potatoes are softened. Garnish with extra thyme and fresh parsley.

HOLIDAY HAM WITH SAGE AND CLOVES

This ham recipe is so easy you'll think you're cheating if you make it for a holiday! Everyone will be amazed that it only takes minutes to prepare but tastes so delicious.

I like to serve the remaining glaze from the slow cooker in a gravy boat with the ham; that way dinner guests can serve themselves if they prefer more on their slice.

My husband's favorite thing about this recipe is making sandwiches with the leftovers! He has been known to request that I make it just so he can slice pieces to take for lunch. It's that good!

Yield: **6–8 SERVINGS**

1 cup (220 g) brown sugar

½ tsp cinnamon

1 tsp ground cloves

1 tsp salt

1½ tsp (1 g) ground sage

2 tbsp (30 ml) spicy brown or whole-grain mustard

½ cup (120 ml) apple juice

½ cup (120 ml) chicken broth

3–5 lb (1.4–2.3 kg) pre-cooked, spiral-cut ham

In a small bowl, combine the brown sugar, cinnamon, cloves, salt, sage, mustard and apple juice. Pour the chicken broth into the slow cooker. Place the ham in the slow cooker. Pour all of the brown sugar glaze over the ham, being sure to get it in between the layers of ham. Cook for 4 hours on high or 8 hours on low. I recommend glazing the ham periodically throughout the cooking process. It really helps flavor every slice. Finish the ham with a final brush of the glaze from the bottom of the slow cooker and let it rest for 10 minutes before slicing and serving.

WHITE WINE PORK CHOPS

White wine and pork chops are a beautiful pairing. All the flavors are evenly matched, which works in this recipe because pork chops are a mild-flavored meat. It's easy for flavors to become muddled in the slow cooker, but this recipe keeps them simple and defined. You will also be amazed by how easy these pork chops are to prepare.

Browning the meat adds a subtle layer of flavor that is important to the final taste of the dish.

Yield: **4–6 SERVINGS**

1 tbsp (15 ml) olive oil

4 pork chops

½ tsp salt

¼ tsp pepper

1 cup (240 ml) chicken broth

½ cup (120 ml) white wine

1 clove garlic, minced

1 cup (240 ml) heavy cream

2 tbsp (3 g) fresh basil, chopped

1 tbsp (4 g) fresh parsley, chopped

Heat the olive oil in a skillet over high heat. Season the pork chops with the salt and pepper. Sear the pork chops on both sides for about 2 minutes per side.

In the slow cooker, combine the chicken broth, white wine and garlic. Nestle the seared pork chops into the liquid.

Cook on high for 4 hours or low for 8 hours. Add the heavy cream, basil and parsley and gently stir to combine. Cook for an additional 30 minutes on low.

EASY PORK CHOPS AND PEPPERS

This is another one of my favorite all-in-one meals! I love just throwing everything together in the slow cooker and letting it do the rest of the work.

My kids love peppers and mushrooms, so this recipe is a particular favorite for them. They enjoy choosing the colors of peppers that we will put in the slow cooker. Letting kids help with meal prep gets them excited to eat and motivates them to try new things! Give it a try when prepping this recipe.

Yield: **4–6 SERVINGS**

1 yellow bell pepper, sliced thin

1 green bell pepper, sliced thin

1 cup (150 g) cherry tomatoes

½ cup (35 g) thin-sliced mushrooms

4 cloves garlic, minced

6 pork chops

2 tbsp (30 ml) balsamic vinegar

1 cup (240 ml) beef or chicken broth

½ tsp salt

¼ tsp pepper

2 tbsp (28 g) butter, cold

2 tsp (4 g) fresh parsley, chopped

2 tsp (1 g) fresh basil, chopped

In the slow cooker, combine the bell peppers, tomatoes, mushrooms and garlic. Set the pork chops on the top of the vegetables. Add the balsamic vinegar, broth, salt and pepper.

Cook on high for 4 hours or low for 8 hours. Add the butter, parsley and basil. Gently stir until combined.

CREAMY SMOTHERED PORK CHOPS

Creamy smothered pork chops are a good, old-fashioned, rib-sticking dinner. These are perfect to come home to after a long day of work. They are bold, flavorful and filling.

We love to serve these over mashed potatoes or egg noodles. The mushroom sauce is an excellent gravy that makes everything it touches delicious.

Yield: **4–6 SERVINGS**

1 cup (240 ml) chicken broth

2 tbsp (16 g) cornstarch

½ cup (80 g) onion, sliced

1 lb (454 g) baby bella mushrooms, sliced

2 cloves garlic, minced

2 tsp (10 ml) Worcestershire sauce

½ tsp salt

¼ tsp pepper

1 sprig oregano

2 sprigs sage, plus more for garnish

6 pork chops

1 cup (240 ml) heavy cream

In the slow cooker, whisk together the chicken broth and the cornstarch. Add the onion, mushrooms, garlic, Worcestershire sauce, salt, pepper, oregano, sage and pork chops.

Cook on high for 4 hours or low for 8 hours. Add the heavy cream and cook until heated through, about 30 minutes on low. Garnish with extra sage.

NO-PREP SAUSAGE AND PEPPER SANDWICHES

This recipe is a staple at family parties in my house! These sandwiches become a favorite of everyone who tries them, and they are requested again and again. Cooking the sausage and sauce together in the slow cooker lets the Italian flavors from the pork sausage flavor the sauce, making everything even more delicious. I like to serve the sauce in little dishes alongside the sandwiches for dipping.

Yield: **6–8 SERVINGS**

1 (29-oz [822-g]) can tomato sauce

1 (6-oz [170-g]) can tomato paste

¾ cup (180 ml) water

8 mild or hot Italian pork sausages

2 red or green bell peppers, sliced

1 medium yellow onion, sliced

½ tsp salt

¼ tsp pepper

1 sprig oregano

1 tbsp (4 g) parsley, minced

1 tbsp (2 g) basil, minced

8 hoagie rolls

2 tbsp (28 g) butter

1 cup (112 g) mozzarella cheese, shredded

In the slow cooker, combine the tomato sauce, tomato paste and water and whisk until smooth. Add the sausages, bell peppers, onion, salt and pepper, nestling them down into the sauce. Place the sprig of oregano on top.

Cook on high for 3 hours or low for 6 hours. Add the fresh parsley and basil to the sauce and stir briefly.

Split the hoagie rolls and spread the butter evenly between them. Sprinkle with mozzarella cheese.

Place the hoagie rolls facing up on a sheet tray and broil them on high for 2 to 3 minutes, until the hoagie rolls are just browned on the edges and the cheese starts to bubble. Divide the sausage and pepper mixture evenly between the hoagie rolls.

FRENCH ONIONY PORK CHOPS

French Oniony Pork Chops are a twist on the classic French onion soup. Packed with all that same flavor and even the melty cheese on top, these pork chops are sure to please anyone you serve them to. Because this recipe has such strong, bold flavors, you should use a thicker cut pork chop, so the taste of the pork doesn't get buried in everything else that's going on in this recipe.

Yield: **4–6 SERVINGS**

1 cup (240 ml) beef broth

1 tbsp (15 ml) Worcestershire sauce

2 tsp (10 ml) soy sauce

1 tbsp (8 g) cornstarch

4 medium yellow onions, sliced

4 sprigs thyme, plus more for garnish

4 thick-cut pork chops

8 slices Swiss cheese

Whisk together the beef broth, Worcestershire sauce, soy sauce and cornstarch in the slow cooker. Add the onions, thyme and pork chops.

Cook on high for 4 hours or low for 8 hours. Place the slices of cheese evenly over the top of the pork chops and onions. Place the lid back on the slow cooker and cook until the cheese is melted, about 20 minutes on low. Garnish with additional thyme.

GARLIC AND ROSEMARY PORK CHOPS

This recipe is so simple, but it is packed with flavor! I love cooking a vegetable at the same time I cook a protein. This makes dinnertime that much simpler when it comes to putting together a balanced meal. This recipe is a personal favorite of mine. I love the bold flavors of the sauce paired with the green beans and the pork chops.

Yield: **4–6 SERVINGS**

2 tbsp (30 ml) olive oil

6 pork chops

½ tsp salt

¼ tsp pepper

¼ tsp red pepper flakes

1 cup (240 ml) chicken broth

4 cloves garlic, whole

4 sprigs rosemary

12 oz (340 g) fresh green beans

4 tbsp (56 g) butter

Mashed potatoes, for serving

Heat the olive oil in a skillet over high heat. Season the pork chops with the salt and pepper. Sear the pork chops for 2 minutes on each side. Place them in the slow cooker with the red pepper flakes, chicken broth, garlic and rosemary.

Cook on high for 3 hours or low for 7 hours. Nestle the green beans in around the pork chops and add the butter. Cook for an additional hour on low. Serve with mashed potatoes.

HONEY MUSTARD PORK ROAST

This pork roast is an all-in-one meal that is easy to throw together but looks impressive when served! The flavors are paired perfectly to be sweet with a little tang and an underlying hint of rosemary.

I love serving this recipe plated on a large platter with the roast sliced in the middle of the platter and the vegetables placed around the outside. This lets everyone eating at the table easily serve themselves while still keeping the presentation a little more formal.

Yield: **6–8 SERVINGS**

2 tbsp (30 ml) olive oil

4–5 lb (1.8–2.3 kg) pork loin roast

½ tsp salt

¼ tsp pepper

2 cloves garlic, minced

2 tbsp (30 ml) Dijon mustard

2 tbsp (30 ml) honey

1 tbsp (3 g) dried rosemary

1 medium yellow onion, quartered

1 lb (454 g) small red or gold potatoes

3 carrots, roughly chopped

1 large apple, any kind, cored and chopped

2 cups (480 ml) chicken broth

Heat the olive oil in a skillet over high heat. Season the pork roast with the salt and pepper. Sear the pork roast on both sides, about 2 minutes per side.

In a small bowl, combine the garlic, mustard, honey and rosemary. Spread the mixture over the seared pork roast.

Add the onion, potatoes, carrots and apple to the slow cooker. Place the pork roast on top of the other ingredients in the slow cooker. Pour the chicken broth around the roast and on top of the vegetables.

Cook on high for 4 hours or low for 8 hours.

APPLE AND SAUERKRAUT PORK ROAST

This recipe was a classic in my house growing up, and I loved converting it into a slow cooker recipe. Slow cooking simplifies the process and ensures that every bite of pork has the flavor of the sauerkraut, apples and onions.

If your family is nervous about trying sauerkraut, that's fine! The pork is delicious even if you don't want to give the sauerkraut a try. But trust me when I tell you that it's delicious! Sauerkraut is fermented cabbage, so while it has a tart smell, the flavor isn't quite as biting. Slow cooking it with sweet apples really tempers the flavors. The pork brings it all together in a delicious medley.

Yield: **6–8 SERVINGS**

2 tbsp (30 ml) olive oil

4–5 lb (1.8–2.3 kg) pork loin roast

½ tsp salt

¼ tsp pepper

I large apple, any kind, cored and sliced thin, plus additional apple wedges, for serving

I medium yellow onion, sliced thin

I tsp fennel seeds, ground

2 cups (284 g) sauerkraut

I cup (240 ml) apple juice

½ cup (120 ml) chicken or vegetable broth

I tbsp (4 g) fresh parsley, minced, for garnish

Heat the olive oil in a skillet over high heat. Season the pork roast with the salt and pepper. Sear the pork roast on both sides, about 2 minutes per side.

Add the apple, onion, fennel seeds, sauerkraut, apple juice and broth to the slow cooker and stir to combine. Add the pork roast on top.

Cook on high for 4 hours or low for 8 hours. Garnish with the fresh parsley and additional apple wedges.

CHEESY MEXICAN PORK CHOPS

This recipe is such a great all-in-one meal. It has protein, veggies and lots of flavor. To fit all of the chops on top of the other ingredients, you'll have to layer them in the slow cooker. They actually cook better this way, as the layering keeps them from drying out.

You can use any kind of cheese you like. We love Colby Jack, but if you prefer a little bit more spice, pepper Jack is also a great option. If you don't have shredded cheese, just use slices. They will melt just fine on top of the pork chops.

Yield: **4–6 SERVINGS**

1 (15.5-oz [439-g]) can black beans, drained and rinsed

1 large tomato, chopped

1 (15.25-oz [432-g]) can corn, drained

1 jalapeño pepper, seeds and membranes removed, minced

½ cup (80 g) red onion, minced

1 clove garlic, minced

1 tbsp (8 g) chili powder

1 tsp cumin

1 sprig oregano

1 tsp salt

1 cup (240 ml) chicken or vegetable broth

6 pork chops

1 cup (100 g) Colby Jack cheese, shredded

1 tbsp (1 g) cilantro

Combine the black beans, tomato, corn, jalapeño, onion, garlic, chili powder, cumin, oregano, salt and broth in the slow cooker. Nestle the pork chops into the mixture in the slow cooker.

Cook on high for 2 hours or low for 6 hours. Sprinkle the cheese on top of the pork chops and cover. Cook until the cheese is melted, about 30 minutes on low. Garnish with cilantro.

SALSA VERDE PORK BITES

This recipe is so simple and easy you'll be amazed at how flavorful it turns out to be! It's spicy and sweet with a little bit of cream—the perfect combination in my book. We enjoy eating this in taco form, in taco salad or over rice. My kids love it no matter how it is served!

You can use any kind of pork roast in this recipe. This recipe is great for less expensive cuts that have a tendency to be tough, because you not only cook it for a long time, but the pieces are small. The small pieces really take on the flavor of the sauce so the flavor gets packed into every bite.

Yield: **4–6 SERVINGS**

2–3 lb (908 g–1.4 kg) pork shoulder roast, cut into 2-inch (5-cm) cubes

2 cups (480 ml) salsa verde (see Note)

¼ cup (60 ml) honey

¼ cup (60 ml) lime juice

¼ cup (60 ml) chicken broth

½ cup (120 ml) heavy cream

¼ cup (4 g) fresh cilantro, chopped

2 avocados, sliced

Combine the pork pieces, salsa verde, honey, lime juice and chicken broth in the slow cooker.

Cook on high for 4 hours or low for 8 hours. Add the heavy cream and cook for an additional 30 minutes on low, until heated through. Stir in the fresh cilantro and serve with sliced avocado.

Note: You can use the salsa verde recipe on page 66, or you can keep things simple and use your favorite store-bought salsa verde.

APPROACHABLE LAMB RECIPES

Lamb is one of our family's favorite proteins. We raise lamb on our farm from our flock of Icelandic Sheep. We see the process from birth to harvest, and being able to open my freezer and have a stock of meat fills me with gratitude.

I love introducing people to lamb. It is a delicious meat and can be easy to prepare. Making it in the slow cooker is a great way to get comfortable with lamb recipes. We actually decided to raise sheep because it was so hard to find lamb where we lived.

Because lamb isn't a protein that most people commonly cook with, I wanted the recipes in this section to be approachable. Every recipe in this chapter is a great way to learn how to cook lamb.

The flavors in these recipes are strong because lamb pairs really well with bold-tasting ingredients. Preparing lamb in the slow cooker is a great way to meld all of the flavors of a dish together. This gives you an end product that is cooked to perfection and tastes amazing, too. I can't wait for you to give some of these recipes a try and discover your own love for lamb!

ROAST LAMB WITH MINTY BUTTER SAUCE

While mint is not a common herb in American cooking, it is a common herb when it comes to cooking lamb. If you've never tried it before, it is delicious. It doesn't make food taste like mint chewing gum, don't worry! The butter sauce is lighter than a gravy and, combined with the mint, gives a really fresh edge that brightens up the lamb's robust flavor. This recipe is perfect with mashed potatoes.

Yield: **6 SERVINGS**

FOR THE LAMB

2–3 lb (908 g–1.4 kg) lamb roast, shoulder or leg

1 tsp salt

½ tsp pepper

2 cloves garlic, minced

2 cups (480 ml) beef broth

FOR THE BUTTER SAUCE

¼ cup (56 g) butter

2 tbsp (3 g) fresh mint, minced

1 tbsp (4 g) fresh parsley, minced

Place the lamb roast in the slow cooker and season it with the salt and pepper. Add the garlic and beef broth around the lamb roast.

Cook on high for 4 hours or low for 8 hours.

When the lamb roast is finished cooking, heat the butter, mint and parsley in a skillet. When the butter is melted and bubbly, about 2 minutes, turn off the heat. Drizzle the lamb roast with the butter sauce for serving.

LAMB MEATBALLS AND MARINARA SAUCE

This recipe is a family classic that I've adapted for lamb. My grandmother was taught to make these meatballs by her grandmother, who moved to America from Italy later in her life. She traditionally used veal to make her meatballs, but that was difficult for my grandmother to find, so she used beef.

I've made these meatballs with a variety of proteins, and lamb is by far my favorite. The lamb is tender, and the texture is so smooth. The lamb pairs deliciously with the other flavors in the meatballs and sauce. This recipe is my husband's all-time favorite and he always sneaks at least four meatballs out of the slow cooker before it's even time for dinner!

Yield: **6 SERVINGS**

FOR THE MEATBALLS
¾ cup (81 g) plain breadcrumbs

2 cloves garlic, grated

¼ cup (60 ml) heavy cream

¼ cup (60 g) ricotta cheese

1 lb (454 g) ground lamb

1 egg

1 tbsp (4 g) dried onion (or 2 tsp [5 g] onion powder)

3 tbsp (5 g) fresh basil, minced

1½ tbsp (6 g) fresh parsley, minced

1 tsp salt

½ tsp pepper

FOR THE MARINARA SAUCE
1 (28-oz [794-g]) can crushed tomatoes

1 (28-oz [794-g]) can tomato sauce

1 (6-oz [170-g]) can tomato paste

¾ cup (180 ml) water

2 tbsp (25 g) sugar

½ cup (80 g) chopped yellow onion

2 cloves garlic, minced

½ tsp salt

¼ tsp pepper

2 tsp (1 g) dried parsley

1 tsp dried basil

½ tsp dried oregano

1 lb (454 g) cooked spaghetti

3 tbsp (15 g) Parmesan cheese, for garnish

Preheat the broiler. Line a broiler pan or sheet tray with parchment paper or spray with cooking spray.

To make the meatballs, in a small bowl, mix the breadcrumbs, garlic, heavy cream and ricotta until evenly combined. Set aside. While the mixture rests, in a large bowl, combine the ground lamb with the egg, dried onion, basil, parsley, salt and pepper and mix until just combined. Add the breadcrumb mixture to the lamb mixture and stir well until everything is combined. The texture should be slightly sticky and moist, not too dry and not too wet. Shape the meatballs so they are roughly the same size. For 25 to 30 meatballs, use about 1 tablespoon (8 g) of mixture per meatball.

Place the meatballs on the prepared pan. Broil the meatballs on high for about 10 minutes or until they are nicely browned on top.

To make the marinara, combine the tomatoes, tomato sauce, tomato paste, water, sugar, onion, garlic, salt, pepper, parsley, basil and oregano in the slow cooker. Add the meatballs to the sauce.

Cook on high for 2 hours or low for 4 hours. Serve with spaghetti and garnish with the Parmesan cheese.

*See image on page 100.

EASY LEG OF LAMB

This leg of lamb recipe is a no-fuss favorite in our house. It takes me only a few minutes to toss all of the ingredients into the slow cooker, and by the end of the day we have an amazing dinner.

Lamb leg roasts are typically larger than lamb shoulder roasts, and they work well in this recipe. The larger cut of meat ensures we will have enough for leftovers the next day. This recipe also makes great sandwiches!

Yield: **6 SERVINGS**

1 medium yellow onion, quartered

3 carrots, sliced into 1–2-inch (3–5-cm) pieces

2 lb (907 g) potatoes, baby or fingerling

2–3 lb (908 g–1.4 kg) leg of lamb roast

½ tsp salt

¼ tsp pepper

2 cloves garlic, minced

¼ cup (60 ml) red wine

2 cups (480 ml) beef broth

2 sprigs rosemary

2 tbsp (8 g) fresh parsley, minced, for garnish

Place the onion, carrots and potatoes in the slow cooker. Place the lamb roast on top of the vegetables in the slow cooker and season it with the salt and pepper. Add the garlic, wine, beef broth and rosemary around the leg of lamb.

Cook on high for 4 hours or low for 8 hours. Garnish with the fresh parsley.

CLASSIC LAMB TIKKA MASALA

Tikka masala is the recipe that started everything with our sheep! This recipe is a favorite of ours at a local restaurant. I tried and tried to re-create it at home with chicken, but it just was not the same. I had such a hard time finding lamb to purchase that I decided to add sheep to our farm.

Even after I started using lamb for this recipe, it still wasn't turning out quite right. I finally figured out that the key was slow cooking. The flavors need to be deep and well blended, which is something the slow cooker does naturally. The coconut milk also gives it another subtle layer of flavor, and while you can use cream instead, I highly recommend you use the coconut milk.

Yield: 6 SERVINGS

FOR THE MARINADE

½ cup (120 ml) plain Greek yogurt

4 cloves garlic, minced

1 tbsp (7 g) garam masala

½ tsp cumin

½ tsp coriander

½ tsp salt

¼ tsp pepper

2–3 lb (908 g–1.4 kg) lamb roast, cubed into 1-inch (3-cm) pieces (see Notes)

FOR THE SAUCE

½ cup (80 g) minced yellow onion

2 cloves garlic, minced

1 tbsp (7 g) garam masala

1 tbsp (6 g) ginger, freshly grated

1 cup (240 ml) coconut milk

1 (15-oz [425-g]) can tomato sauce

1 bay leaf

1 green bell pepper, chopped

4 cups (744) cooked rice, for serving

Combine the Greek yogurt, garlic, garam masala, cumin, coriander, salt and pepper in the slow cooker. Add the lamb to the marinade and stir until it is completely coated.

Cook on high for 1 hour.

Add the onion, garlic, garam masala, ginger, coconut milk, tomato sauce, bay leaf and bell pepper to the slow cooker. Stir until everything is well combined and smooth.

Cook on high for 3 hours or low for 6 hours. Serve over rice.

Notes: You can use lamb stew meat in place of the cubed lamb roast. You can also marinate the lamb overnight in the refrigerator if that fits your schedule better; after marinating, simply follow the rest of the recipe as directed.

DUMP-AND-GO BBQ LAMB RIBS

This is perhaps the easiest recipe in this entire cookbook—and with the fewest ingredients! It takes less than five minutes to put together, but the outcome is packed with flavor. I have cooked many different kinds of ribs in the slow cooker, but lamb ribs always win out for me. There is something about their smaller size that just does a better job of taking on the flavor of the sauce while slow cooking. Usually when you make ribs, you only use one rack, or one side of the ribs. With lamb ribs, I always use two racks because they are smaller.

Yield: **6 SERVINGS**

2 racks of lamb ribs, bone-in

1 (18-oz [530-ml]) bottle BBQ sauce

½ cup (120 ml) water

1 bay leaf

Pickles, for serving

Combine the lamb ribs, BBQ sauce, water and bay leaf in the slow cooker.

Cook on high for 4 hours or low for 8 hours. Rotate the ribs periodically so that every rib has a chance at the bottom of the slow cooker in the sauce. Serve with pickles.

PULLED LAMB SHOULDER WITH CREAMY COLESLAW

I love pulled lamb and slaw, and this recipe is so tasty. The lamb is slightly spicy and very tender with a great texture. It pairs really well with the creamy coleslaw, and the cilantro brightens everything up.

We eat this recipe on sandwiches or just plain with the coleslaw on the side. Whichever way you eat it, you won't be disappointed.

Yield: **6 SERVINGS**

FOR THE LAMB ROAST
1 tsp salt

½ tsp pepper

2 tsp (4 g) cumin

1 tbsp (8 g) chili powder

1 tsp ground coriander

2 tsp (5 g) paprika

3 cloves garlic, minced

1 medium yellow onion, halved

2–3 lb (908 g–1.4 kg) lamb shoulder roast

1½ cups (360 ml) beef broth

FOR THE CREAMY COLESLAW
½ head green cabbage, sliced thin or shredded

1 cup (110 g) grated carrot

⅓ cup (16 g) scallions, sliced thin

½ cup (8 g) cilantro, chopped

1 cup (240 ml) mayonnaise

1 tbsp (15 ml) apple cider vinegar

1 tbsp (12 g) sugar

½ tsp salt

¼ tsp black pepper

For the lamb roast, in a small bowl, combine the salt, pepper, cumin, chili powder, coriander, paprika and garlic. Place the onion in the bottom of the slow cooker. Place the lamb roast on top of the onion. Sprinkle the seasoning over the lamb roast. Pour the beef broth around the lamb roast.

Cook the lamb roast on high for 4 hours or low for 8 hours.

For the coleslaw, in a large bowl, toss the cabbage, carrot, scallions and cilantro. In a smaller bowl, whisk together the mayonnaise, apple cider vinegar, sugar, salt and pepper. Pour the mayonnaise mixture over top of the cabbage mixture and toss everything together.

MUSTARD AND THYME LAMB CHOPS

I love all of the flavors in these lamb chops so much. Lamb pairs so well with the tang of stone-ground mustard and the savory edge from the garlic and herbs. This is a one-pot meal that is packed with flavor!

Most of the time I hear hesitation when it comes to eating lamb chops, because they are best served rare when you cook them in a pan or on the grill. If you prepare them in a slow cooker, you still get that great flavor from the lamb chops, but they become nice and tender in the slow cooker, so you get the best of both worlds.

Yield: **6 SERVINGS**

3 tbsp (42 g) butter, softened

2 tbsp (30 ml) stone-ground mustard

4 cloves garlic, minced

1 tbsp (3 g) fresh thyme, minced, plus more for garnish

1 tsp ground sage

6–8 lamb chops

2 lb (907 g) small red or yellow potatoes, whole

1¾ cups (420 ml) beef broth

In a small bowl, combine the butter, mustard, garlic, thyme and sage. Smear the mixture evenly over the lamb chops. Place the potatoes in the slow cooker and pour the beef broth over them. Add the lamb chops on top.

Cook on high for 2 hours or low for 4 hours. Garnish with additional thyme.

FOOLPROOF SHEPHERD'S PIE

This is a classic recipe made even better in the slow cooker! I love how slow cooking the base ingredients really melds the flavors. Even though this isn't baked in the oven, the mashed potatoes still get nice and crisp on the edges. The melted butter and parsley on top at the end really brighten up the remaining flavors in the dish and bring it all together nicely.

Yield: **6 SERVINGS**

1 lb (454 g) ground lamb

¼ cup (30 g) flour

2 red or gold potatoes, cubed

1 carrot, chopped

1 celery stalk, chopped

1 (6-oz [170-g]) can tomato paste

2 cups (480 ml) beef broth

½ cup (80 g) minced yellow onion

½ tsp salt

¼ tsp pepper

½ cup (65 g) frozen peas

2 tsp (2 g) fresh rosemary, minced

1 tsp thyme, fresh, minced

3 cups (630 g) mashed potatoes, prepared (instant or fresh)

2 tbsp (28 g) butter, cubed

2 tbsp (8 g) fresh parsley, minced, for garnish

In a skillet over medium heat, brown the ground lamb, about 5 to 7 minutes. Add the browned meat to the slow cooker, along with the flour, and stir until the lamb is evenly coated. Add the cubed potatoes, carrot, celery, tomato paste, beef broth, onion, salt, pepper, peas, rosemary and thyme. Stir until the ingredients are all well combined.

Cook on high for 3 hours or low for 7 hours. Smooth the top and spread the mashed potatoes evenly over the top of the ingredients in the slow cooker. Dot the top with the butter. Replace the lid and cook for an additional 30 minutes on high or 1 hour on low. Garnish with the parsley.

LAMB GYROS AND HOMEMADE TZATZIKI SAUCE

The first time I ever had a gyro was from a Greek street food vendor in Washington, DC, when I was visiting my uncle. To say that set my bar really high for how gyros should taste is an understatement! Every gyro I've had since then has failed to measure up, so I decided to try making them myself.

I really wanted those Greek flavors to shine through in the roast. I also wanted the tzatziki sauce to be fresh and full of flavor, which is why it's really important to use fresh herbs. I am so pleased with how this recipe turned out. I may just need to go back to DC and see if I can do a taste comparison!

Yield: **6 SERVINGS**

FOR THE LAMB
2 lb (907 g) lamb roast (leg or shoulder)

3 cloves garlic, minced

1 medium yellow onion, quartered

2 tsp (1 g) dried rosemary

1 tsp dried oregano

½ tsp salt

¼ tsp pepper

2 tbsp (30 ml) lemon juice

1 cup (240 ml) water

FOR THE TZATZIKI SAUCE
1½ cups (360 ml) plain Greek yogurt

2 tbsp (30 ml) lemon juice

2 tsp (1 g) fresh dill, minced

1 tsp fresh mint, minced

1 clove garlic, minced

½ tsp salt

¼ tsp pepper

1 cup (100 g) minced cucumber

FOR SERVING
6 fresh pitas, warmed

½ cup (75 g) cherry tomatoes, sliced

1 red onion, chopped

Combine the lamb, garlic, onion, rosemary, oregano, salt, pepper, lemon juice and water in the slow cooker.

Cook on high for 4 hours or low for 8 hours.

To make the tzatziki sauce, in a medium bowl, combine the Greek yogurt, lemon juice, dill, mint, garlic, salt, pepper and cucumber. Let the mixture sit in the refrigerator for a few hours so the flavors can meld.

To serve, thinly slice the lamb and place it in a pita. Top with the tzatziki sauce, tomatoes and onion.

TANGY LAMB MEATLOAF

Lamb meatloaf is one of our favorite recipes. It's flavorful, tangy and easy to cook in the slow cooker! There is no extra liquid in this recipe, which can seem crazy, but it works.

This recipe is unique to our family. With a freezer full of lamb, I had to get creative, and this is one of the amazing recipes I came up with for my family—it was a hit! We love this meatloaf with mashed potatoes.

Yield: **6 SERVINGS**

FOR THE MEATLOAF
¼ cup (60 ml) milk

I slice bread, torn into I-inch (3-cm) pieces

I lb (454 g) ground lamb

½ cup (80 g) minced yellow onion

2 cloves garlic, minced

2 tsp (I g) dried rosemary

½ tsp dried thyme

I tsp dried basil

½ tsp salt

I egg

FOR THE SAUCE
¾ cup (180 ml) ketchup

I tbsp (14 g) brown sugar

½ tsp onion powder

½ tsp garlic powder

¼ tsp dried mustard

2 tsp (10 ml) Worcestershire sauce

To make the meatloaf, pour the milk in a shallow dish or bowl. Add the torn bread and let it sit for a few minutes. In a large bowl, combine the milk-soaked bread with the lamb, onion, garlic, rosemary, thyme, basil, salt and egg and stir until the ingredients are thoroughly mixed.

Fold a piece of parchment paper so that it goes down one side of the slow cooker and up the other. This creates a sling that will make it easy to get the meatloaf out. Place the meatloaf mix into the slow cooker, on top of the parchment paper, then pat it into a loaf form.

Cook the meatloaf on high for 3 hours or low for 6 hours.

To make the sauce, combine the ketchup, brown sugar, onion powder, garlic powder, mustard and Worcestershire sauce. Pour the sauce over the top of the meatloaf and continue to cook on high for 30 minutes or low for I hour.

HEARTY SOUPS AND STEWS

There is something about a hearty soup or stew that warms your soul as well as your belly. I love preparing every one of these recipes for my family on chilly days. There is nothing more comforting than coming in from the cold to the smell of soup in the slow cooker.

Many of the ingredients in these recipes are things I've grown in my garden and stored for the winter. There is something very satisfying about making a meal almost entirely with ingredients you've grown and raised yourself. It makes these recipes feel even more personal and reminds me that the dark, chilly days of fall and winter will eventually fade to spring and the whole cycle of life and growing food for my family will begin again.

Because we also raise meat on our farm, these recipes are also reminders of that same cycle of life for our animals. Being able to raise our own meat fills me with gratitude every time I make a meal. When you raise your own meat, you get every part of the animal, which results in some cuts of meat that aren't very tender. Slow cooking them in soups and stews is a perfect way to use these otherwise tough pieces of meat and still get all the delicious flavor and taste out of them.

WINTER VEGETABLE CHOWDER WITH AGED CHEDDAR

This winter vegetable chowder is one of my favorite recipes. It is warm, filling and comforting while remaining fresh at the same time. This recipe is really easy to put together; making the roux for the creamy sauce isn't hard. A roux is a mixture of fat and flour, typically in a 1:1 ratio. I like to use butter for this soup because it adds another layer of flavor to the chowder.

I often have broccoli and cauliflower from my garden stashed away in the freezer, so I love using that if I don't have access to fresh. You can use fresh or frozen broccoli and cauliflower in this recipe. I've used both, and it turns out beautifully either way.

Yield: **6–8 SERVINGS**

3 tbsp (42 g) butter

3 tbsp (25 g) flour

4 cups (960 ml) vegetable broth

½ tsp salt

¼ tsp pepper

1 cup (145 g) corn

1 cup (128 g) chopped carrots

½ cup (60 g) diced celery

½ cup (80 g) diced yellow onion

3 cups (450 g) diced red or gold potatoes

½ cup (45 g) broccoli

½ cup (55 g) cauliflower

1 tsp dried parsley

1 cup (240 ml) heavy cream

1 cup (240 ml) half and half

1 tbsp (3 g) fresh chives

2 tsp (1 g) fresh thyme

1 cup (110 g) aged Cheddar cheese, grated, for garnish

In a medium saucepan over medium heat, melt the butter. Add the flour and stir until it is well combined. Cook the mixture for 1 to 2 minutes, then add the vegetable broth, salt and pepper. Whisk the flour and broth mixture until it is well combined, then remove from the heat.

Add the broth mixture, corn, carrots, celery, onion, potatoes, broccoli, cauliflower and parsley to the slow cooker. Stir until everything is combined.

Cook on high for 4 hours or low for 6 hours.

Add the heavy cream, half and half, chives and thyme. Stir until well combined. Cook the chowder for an additional 30 minutes, up to 1 hour on low heat. Garnish with the cheese.

GARDEN BUTTERNUT SQUASH SOUP

Would you believe it if I told you I'd never eaten a butternut squash before I grew one in my garden? It's true! I love growing things I haven't ever eaten or haven't eaten often, because it gives me a great excuse to try something new. I became hooked on squash of all kinds after growing a giant patch of them, but there is something so perfect about the flavor of a butternut squash. The sweet balanced with the savory of this dish is delicious, and the fresh sage sends the flavor of the butternut squash out of this world.

If you've never made browned butter before, this is a great way to learn! By browning the butter with a sage leaf in it, you are infusing the sage flavor into the butter. So not only do you get the amazing nutty flavor from the browned butter, but you get the flavor of the sage as well! It's the perfect way to finish off this soup.

Yield: **4–6 SERVINGS**

1 butternut squash

1 cup (160 g) diced yellow onion

6 cups (1.4 L) vegetable or chicken broth

½ tsp salt

¼ tsp pepper

2 sprigs plus 2 tsp (1 g) fresh thyme, divided

5 fresh sage leaves, divided

1 cup (240 ml) heavy cream

4 tbsp (56 g) butter

Peel the butternut squash. Trim off both ends, then cut the squash in half to separate the skinnier neck from the wider bottom. Cut both sections in half lengthwise. Remove the seeds and then dice the squash into 1-inch (3-cm) cubes. Add the squash, onion and vegetable broth to the slow cooker, then add the salt, pepper, 2 sprigs of thyme and 3 of the sage leaves and stir to combine.

Cook on high for 3 hours or low for 6 hours. Blend the soup in a blender, food processor or with an immersion blender. If you use a blender or food processor, be very careful! Hot liquids expand, so only fill the machine to half full. Return the soup to the slow cooker and add the heavy cream. The consistency should be thick but slide in a stream off of a spoon. Thin with additional broth or water if needed.

On the stovetop in a small skillet over medium heat, warm the butter until it is melted. Add the remaining 2 sage leaves to the melted butter. Continue to stir until the butter bubbles and the butterfat solids start to brown. As soon as they start to brown, remove the butter from the heat and discard the sage leaves. Be careful: Butter can burn easily!

Garnish the soup with the browned butter and the remaining fresh thyme.

NO-PREP LAMB AND POTATO STEW

One of my favorite things about living on a farm is being able to make a recipe almost completely from ingredients we raised ourselves—it feels so satisfying. This soup represents that feeling for me, and eating it is not only delicious, but it fills me with a sense of gratitude and pride in all of our hard work.

The flavors in this stew are deep and robust. One complaint I often hear about cooking with lamb is that it can be tough. I have never found this to be the case, especially when using a slow cooker. This recipe turns out perfectly tender and flavorful every single time.

Yield: **6 SERVINGS**

1 lb (454 g) lamb stew meat

1 cup (160 g) diced yellow onion

2 medium red potatoes, diced into 1-inch (3-cm) pieces

1 cup (128 g) diced carrots

1 cup (120 g) diced celery

½ tsp dried oregano

½ tsp dried parsley

½ tsp ground sage

2 tsp (5 g) cornstarch

½ tsp salt

¼ tsp pepper

1 (15-oz [425-g]) can diced tomatoes

6 cups (1.4 L) beef broth

1 cup (130 g) frozen peas

Combine the lamb, onion, potatoes, carrots, celery, oregano, parsley, sage, cornstarch, salt and pepper in the slow cooker. Stir the ingredients so that all of the ingredients are coated with the cornstarch. Add the tomatoes and stir until all the ingredients are well combined. Add the beef broth and stir again until everything is combined.

Cook on high for 4 hours or low for 8 hours. Add the peas and stir until combined. Let sit, covered, for about 5 minutes.

CREAMY KALE AND SAUSAGE SOUP

This soup is one of my favorites to make. I love the way kale cooks in the slow cooker:
It holds its flavor and bite while still cooking down enough to blend well with the dish.
I always grow way too much kale in my garden and have bags of it stored in my freezer.
This is a great way to use it up and get some easy veggies into dinner.

It's important to add the cream at the end of the cooking time. Slow cooker recipes are
cooked for too long to be able to add the cream at the beginning without it breaking
down. It doesn't take long at all to heat through after you've added it in. Add the
cream and by the time you get everyone settled for dinner, it will be ready!

Yield: **6 SERVINGS**

1 tbsp (15 ml) olive oil

1 lb (454 g) mild Italian sausage

¼ tsp red pepper flakes

⅛ tsp nutmeg

2 cloves garlic, minced

6 small red potatoes, sliced

4 cups (960 ml) beef broth

½ tsp salt

½ tsp pepper

2 cups (480 ml) heavy cream

2 cups packed (150 g) chopped kale

1 tbsp (2 g) fresh basil, minced

2 tbsp (8 g) fresh parsley, minced

¼ cup (20 g) Parmesan cheese, grated, for garnish

In a small skillet, heat the olive oil over medium heat until it
shimmers. Add the sausage and cook it until it is browned, 5 to 7
minutes. Add the browned sausage, red pepper flakes, nutmeg,
garlic, potatoes, beef broth, salt and pepper to the slow cooker.

Cook on high for 3 hours or low for 6 hours.

Add the heavy cream, kale, basil and parsley. Stir the soup to
combine and replace the lid. Cook the soup on low for an
additional 30 minutes, until the kale is softened and the cream
is warmed. Garnish the soup with the Parmesan cheese.

HEARTY CHICKEN SOUP WITH HOMEMADE NOODLES

This soup is a childhood favorite. Growing up, my mother would make soup every Wednesday night for dinner. This was my mom's signature soup, and she would often ask me to make the homemade noodles to make it extra special. I learned to make these noodles from my grandmother on my father's side, and it is a fond memory we have together in the kitchen. I can remember rolling them out with her weathered hands on top of mine and her patience with my childish cutting skills. She let me do everything in the kitchen and taught me so much. The soup recipe isn't just dinner to me; it's part of who I am.

Yield: **4–6 SERVINGS**

FOR THE SOUP

1 cup (128 g) diced carrots

½ cup (60 g) diced celery

½ cup (80 g) diced yellow onion

½ tsp salt

¼ tsp pepper

1 cup (225 g) canned diced tomatoes

4 cups (960 ml) chicken broth

4 cups (960 ml) water

1 tsp or 1 cube chicken bouillon

3 chicken thighs, boneless and skinless

1 sprig thyme

2 tsp (3 g) fresh parsley

FOR THE NOODLES

1 egg

2 tbsp (30 ml) water

½ tsp salt

½ tsp baking powder

1 tsp fresh parsley, minced

½–1 cup (63–126 g) all-purpose flour, plus more for rolling

To make the soup, add the carrots, celery, onion, salt, pepper, tomatoes, chicken broth, water and chicken bouillon to the slow cooker. Stir the ingredients to combine. Nestle the chicken thighs into the slow cooker. Add the sprig of thyme.

Cook on high for 3 hours or low for 6 hours.

While the soup is cooking, prepare the noodles. Combine the egg and water in a medium bowl. Add the salt, baking powder, parsley and ½ cup (63 g) of the flour. Stir until all of the ingredients are combined. Continue adding flour until a soft, dry dough forms. Smooth the dough into a ball and cover it with plastic wrap. Let the dough rest for 30 minutes at room temperature, or up to overnight in the refrigerator.

Roll the dough out on a lightly floured surface until it is about ⅛ inch (3 mm) thick. Slice the dough into ¼- to ½-inch (6- to 13-mm)-wide noodles, or however wide or thin as you would like. Let the noodles dry for 15 minutes or up to 30 minutes.

Remove the chicken from the slow cooker and dice, then add the diced chicken to the slow cooker. Add the dried noodles and fresh parsley to the soup and cook for 30 minutes on high.

CHICKEN STEW WITH ROSEMARY AND THYME DUMPLINGS

This recipe is one of the first recipes I learned to make after I got married. I had never cooked with chicken thighs before, not to mention followed a recipe with so many steps! I have since refined this recipe, simplified it and made it into the slow cooker recipe you see here.

It remains a favorite in our home and brings back fond memories of the tiny apartment we rented after we were married. It was in an old house and the smells of dinner lingered until the next morning. Making this soup also makes me remember the first time I made it in the home we live in now, which somehow made it feel like *our* home instead of just a house.

Yield: **4–6 SERVINGS**

FOR THE CHICKEN STEW

1 cup (128 g) small-dice carrots

⅓ cup (40 g) small-dice celery

½ cup (80 g) small-dice yellow onion

2 cloves garlic, minced

½ tsp salt

¼ tsp pepper

¼ cup (60 ml) white wine (or chicken broth)

1 tbsp (8 g) cornstarch

2 cups (480 ml) chicken broth

5 chicken thighs, boneless and skinless

2 sprigs fresh rosemary

2 sprigs fresh thyme

3 tbsp (42 g) butter

¼ cup (60 ml) heavy cream

¼ cup (60 ml) whole milk

½ cup (65 g) frozen peas

FOR THE DUMPLINGS

1 cup (125 g) all-purpose flour

2 tsp (9 g) baking powder

½ tsp salt

1 tsp fresh rosemary, minced

1 tsp fresh thyme, minced

½ cup (120 ml) whole milk

2 tbsp (30 ml) melted butter

To make the chicken stew, combine the carrots, celery, onion, garlic, salt, pepper and white wine in the slow cooker. In a small bowl, whisk the cornstarch into the chicken broth and add the mixture to the slow cooker. Nestle the chicken thighs into the mixture in the slow cooker. Add the rosemary, thyme and butter on top of the chicken.

Cook on high for 3 hours or low for 6 hours.

While the stew is cooking, make the dumplings. In a medium bowl, combine the flour, baking powder, salt, rosemary and thyme. Add the milk and the melted butter and stir until combined and a loose dough has formed.

At the end of the stew cooking time, remove the chicken thighs and shred the chicken. Add it back into the slow cooker. Add the heavy cream, milk and frozen peas to the slow cooker. Stir to combine. Drop rounded table-spoons (15 g) of the dough onto the stew. Cook the dumplings for an additional hour on high. They will look damp on the edges but will be cooked all the way through on the inside.

*See image on page 122.

DUMP-AND-GO BEEF AND VEGETABLE STEW

This recipe is a refined version of the beef stew we used to eat growing up. My family always had ample food stores, which we relied on heavily when times were tight after my father lost his job. Canned beef stew was something we ate often, and it came to represent resilience to me.

This homemade version always reminds me that preparation for hard times pays off, and that hard times don't last forever. I am always extra grateful for the food on our table when I ladle this stew into everyone's dinner bowls.

Yield: **4–6 SERVINGS**

1 lb (454 g) beef stew meat

1 cup (128 g) diced carrots

1 cup (120 g) diced celery

1 cup (160 g) diced yellow onion

1 cup (130 g) diced parsnips

1 medium red or gold potato, diced

½ tsp ground sage

3 sprigs fresh thyme

2 tsp (5 g) cornstarch

½ tsp salt

¼ tsp pepper

1 (15-oz [425-g]) can diced tomatoes

6 cups (1.4 L) beef broth

1 cup (130 g) frozen peas

Combine the beef stew meat, carrots, celery, onion, parsnips, potato, sage, thyme, cornstarch, salt and pepper in the slow cooker. Stir everything so that the cornstarch coats all the other ingredients. Add the tomatoes and stir until well combined. Add the beef broth and stir again until combined.

Cook on high for 4 hours or low for 8 hours.

Add the peas and stir until combined. Let sit, covered, for about 5 minutes.

EASY-PREP POTATO AND LEEK SOUP

This recipe is one of my all-time favorites! The flavor the leeks give this soup elevates it from traditional potato soup and is so divine. If you have never cooked with a leek before, this is the perfect opportunity.

Leeks are part of the onion family and have a slight anise flavor to them as well. They are grown in very sandy soil, which sometimes gets stuck in the leek, so the easiest way to clean them is to trim the tops and bottom so you're left with the middle portion that is light green and white. Then, slice the leek in half lengthwise and float the halves in water. All the sand will fall out in the water and then you can mince them without fear of grit.

Yield: **6 SERVINGS**

½ cup (80 g) yellow onion, minced

½ cup (60 g) minced celery

2 cups (180 g) minced leeks

6 red or gold potatoes, peeled and roughly chopped

5 cups (1.2 L) chicken broth

1 tsp seasoned salt

½ tsp salt

½ tsp pepper, plus more for serving

3 sprigs fresh thyme

2 cups (480 ml) heavy cream

Olive oil, for serving

2 tbsp (8 g) fresh parsley, chopped

Combine the onion, celery, leeks, potatoes, chicken broth, seasoned salt, salt, pepper and thyme in the slow cooker.

Cook on high for 3 hours or low for 7 hours. Add the heavy cream and let it cook for an additional 30 minutes, or until the soup is warmed through. If desired, blend to a smooth consistency in a blender or with an immersion blender. If you use a blender or food processor, be very careful! Hot liquids expand, so only fill the machine to half full. The soup should be slightly thick but flow off of a spoon easily. Add more broth if needed.

Divide the soup into 6 bowls and drizzle olive oil and sprinkle pepper into each bowl. Garnish with fresh parsley.

AWARD-WINNING BEEF AND LAMB CHILI

I am not lying when I say this chili has won awards! I've shared this recipe with a few people and more than one of them has reported back that they won a chili cook-off with it! I suppose it's time for me to enter some chili cook-offs.

In all seriousness, this chili really is amazing. It is a version of a chili recipe my dad makes when we go camping as a family. It has lots of amazing flavors and is hearty and filling. I tend to make it only slightly spicy, so feel free to up the spice level if you like it hot!

Yield: **6 SERVINGS**

1 lb (454 g) lamb chunks, about 1-inch (3-cm) cubes

1 lb (454 g) beef chunks, about 1-inch (3-cm) cubes

4 cloves garlic, minced

1 jalapeño pepper, minced (see Notes)

1 medium yellow onion, small dice

1 stalk celery, small dice

2 tsp (4 g) cumin

1 tbsp (8 g) chili powder

¼ tsp cayenne (see Notes)

1½ tsp (9 g) salt

3 cups (720 ml) beef broth

2 tbsp (28 g) brown sugar

1 (28-oz [794-g]) can crushed tomatoes

1 (6-oz [170-g]) can tomato paste

1 bay leaf

1 (15-oz [425-g]) can kidney beans, drained and rinsed

1 (15-oz [425-g]) can northern beans, drained and rinsed

¼ cup (4 g) cilantro, fresh, chopped

Add the lamb chunks, beef chunks, garlic, jalapeño, onion, celery, cumin, chili powder, cayenne, salt, beef broth, brown sugar, tomatoes, tomato paste and bay leaf to the slow cooker and stir to combine.

Cook on high for 3 hours or on low for 7 hours.

Add the kidney beans, northern beans and cilantro. Stir to combine and let the chili heat through, about 30 minutes on high.

Notes: You can remove the seeds and membranes from the jalapeño to temper the spiciness. You can also adjust the cayenne pepper measurement to your liking. I usually make this chili with the listed measurements, and I remove the seeds and membranes from the jalapeño. It has a mild spice that way.

SAGE AND PARSLEY CHICKEN AND WILD RICE SOUP

When I developed this recipe, I was looking to make a soup that felt lighter than a typical chicken soup. This recipe turned out just as I wanted it to, and it's actually quite healthy as well as filling.

I like adding the parsley at the end of the cooking time because it really brightens up all of the other flavors. Sometimes slow cooker recipes can taste muddled, and adding fresh herbs at the end really helps define all of the individual flavors in the recipe.

Yield: **6 SERVINGS**

1 cup (128 g) diced carrots

½ cup (60 g) diced celery

½ cup (80 g) diced yellow onion

½ tsp salt

¼ tsp pepper

9 cups (2.1 L) chicken broth

1 tsp or 1 cube chicken bouillon

3 chicken thighs, boneless and skinless

1 bay leaf

3 sprigs fresh sage

1 cup (190 g) wild rice, uncooked

2 tsp (3 g) fresh parsley, minced

Combine the carrots, celery, onion, salt, pepper, chicken broth, chicken bouillon, chicken thighs, bay leaf, sage and wild rice in the slow cooker.

Cook on high for 4 hours or low for 8 hours. Add the fresh parsley and stir to combine.

THYME AND SWISS FRENCH ONION SOUP

If you love French onion soup but need an easier version, this recipe is perfect for you! I love the *idea* of French onion soup but am not as fond of standing in front of the stove for so long and dirtying so many dishes. This soup is not only easy to make in the slow cooker, but it also only uses one pot!

Traditionally, Gruyère cheese is used in this recipe, but I wrote my recipe with Swiss since finding specialty cheeses can be difficult where I live. Either cheese will turn out delicious in this recipe.

Yield: **8 SERVINGS**

6 medium yellow onions, sliced

8 sprigs fresh thyme

4 cups (960 ml) beef broth

3 cups (720 ml) water

½ tsp pepper

3 tbsp (45 ml) Worcestershire sauce

1 tbsp (15 ml) soy sauce

1 tbsp (8 g) cornstarch

8 slices crusty bread

4 tbsp (56 g) butter

8 slices Swiss cheese

Place the onions, thyme, beef broth, water, pepper and Worcestershire sauce in the slow cooker. In a small bowl, whisk together the soy sauce and cornstarch. Add the cornstarch slurry to the slow cooker and stir until well blended.

Cook on high for 4 hours or low for 8 hours.

Near the end of the soup cooking time, butter the bread on both sides. Broil each side for 2 minutes, or until golden brown and toasty. Watch it closely so it doesn't burn!

Place the slices of toasted bread evenly over the top of the soup in the slow cooker. Place the slices of cheese over the top of the slices of bread. Place the lid on the slow cooker and let it cook on high until the cheese is melted, about 10 minutes.

EASY PASTA E FAGIOLI

Pasta e fagioli is one of my favorite soup recipes, because it is so quick to put together. My kids also love eating the tiny noodles, so it's a big hit with them as well!

The pasta really won't take long at all to cook, so it's important to add it right at the end of the cooking time. I like to test pasta to see if it is done by tasting it, and the same rule applies here. Just give the soup a taste test before serving to make sure the noodles are perfectly cooked.

Yield: **6 SERVINGS**

1 cup (128 g) diced carrots

½ cup (80 g) diced yellow onion

½ cup (60 g) diced celery

2 garlic cloves, minced

½ lb (227 g) Italian sausage links, diced

1 (28-oz [794-g]) can crushed tomatoes

6 cups (1.4 L) vegetable broth

1 sprig fresh oregano

1 (15-oz [425-g]) can kidney beans

1 (15-oz [425-g]) can white beans

1½ cups (170 g) ditalini pasta

1 tbsp (2 g) fresh basil, minced

½ tbsp (2 g) fresh parsley, minced

¼ cup (20 g) Parmesan cheese, grated

In the slow cooker, combine the carrots, onion, celery, garlic, sausage, tomatoes, vegetable broth and oregano.

Cook on high for 3 hours or low for 6 hours.

Add the kidney beans, white beans and ditalini pasta.

Cook for an additional 20 minutes on low, or until the pasta is al dente. Add the basil, parsley and Parmesan cheese and stir until combined.

CLASSIC PASTA AND SAUCES

This section of my cookbook is a tribute to my Italian heritage. While I don't claim that any of these recipes are authentic, they are authentically *me*. I grew up eating these recipes at my grandmother's house and my own house. They were present at every family gathering and a staple we knew would always be there. Some of our absolute favorites were macaroni and cheese and lasagna.

These are the recipes that taught me what a pinch, smidge, dash and shake meant. These are the recipes that taught me that you have to taste as you go. Some of my most vivid memories in the kitchen are of making these recipes with my mother, grandmother and aunts. While each of them made these recipes a little differently and everyone had a different name for them, they always turned out delicious. Usually that time together making these recipes was filled with laughter and joy, and the kitchen was one of my happy places as a child.

The recipes in this chapter also taught me that food carries more than nutrition for our bodies: It carries nutrition for our souls. It can bridge gaps and create friends. It can forge family relationships stronger than steel. While sharing the dishes in this chapter my family has laughed together, cried together and everything in between. These are the recipes I grew up on. I know these recipes can help you create happy, beautiful memories with your own family.

HOMESTYLE MACARONI AND CHEESE

This recipe is one I have worked on perfecting for years. I am so excited to share it with you! I love making it in the slow cooker, because it's so much easier than dirtying a lot of dishes and having to use the stovetop and oven.

The tomato paste is my secret ingredient—it doesn't make the macaroni and cheese too tomato-flavored—it just adds a hint of tomato in the background that really enhances all the other flavors. I know this will be a favorite in your house, like it is in ours!

Using a slow cooker liner or lining your slow cooker with foil will make cleanup easy for this recipe.

Yield: **6 SERVINGS**

1 lb (454 g) elbow macaroni, uncooked

1 cup (240 ml) heavy cream

2½ cups (600 ml) chicken broth

1 tbsp (16 g) tomato paste

½ tsp black pepper

⅛ tsp cayenne pepper

¼ tsp salt

¼ tsp seasoned salt

1½ cups (165 g) Cheddar cheese, shredded

1 tbsp (3 g) fresh chives, chopped

Combine the macaroni, cream, chicken broth, tomato paste, black pepper, cayenne pepper, salt and seasoned salt in the slow cooker.

Cook on low for 2 hours or high for 1 hour, until the pasta is tender.

When the pasta is al dente, add the Cheddar cheese and chives. Stir until the cheese is melted.

LEMONY STUFFED MANICOTTI

I have been making this recipe for years! You can use jumbo shells or manicotti, but the manicotti is easier to fill than the shells, because both are not yet cooked when you fill them.

The filling and sauce complement each other beautifully in this dish. Don't be scared to add the lemon zest! It is a delicious flavor and really makes this recipe unique. I love adding spinach to the filling so it's an all-in-one meal! Picky eaters will not even notice, and it's a great way to get in some veggies.

Yield: **6 SERVINGS**

22 oz (624 g) ricotta cheese

I large egg

I cup (80 g) Parmesan cheese, finely grated

2 packed cups (90 g) spinach, finely chopped

I tsp salt

½ tsp pepper

15 manicotti noodles, uncooked

4 cloves garlic, crushed or finely minced

⅛ tsp red pepper flakes

I (28-oz [794-g]) can crushed tomatoes

I cup (240 ml) water

I tbsp (12 g) sugar

2 tsp (4 g) lemon zest, from about I lemon

I tbsp (4 g) fresh parsley, chopped, plus more for garnish

I tbsp (2 g) fresh basil, chopped

I cup (112 g) mozzarella cheese, grated

¼ cup (20 g) Parmesan, coarsely grated

Combine the ricotta, egg, Parmesan cheese, spinach, salt and pepper in a medium bowl. Mix well. Using a piping bag or a zip-top bag with the corner trimmed off, pipe the ricotta mixture evenly between the uncooked manicotti. Set aside.

Combine the garlic, red pepper flakes, tomatoes, water, sugar, lemon zest, parsley and basil in a large bowl. Add half of the sauce to the slow cooker. Place the manicotti in a single layer in the slow cooker. There may be a little bit of overlap but most of the manicotti should be in a single layer. Pour the remaining sauce over the top of the manicotti.

Cook on high for 2 hours or low for 4 hours, until the pasta is tender. Add the mozzarella and the coarsely grated Parmesan cheese to the top of the manicotti and cover until melted, about 15 minutes on low. Garnish with fresh parsley.

Note: Using a slow cooker liner or lining your slow cooker with foil will make cleanup easy for this recipe.

CREAMY CHICKEN ALFREDO

If you know me, you know that I love creamy pasta sauces. I would make creamy pasta sauces every day if my family would tolerate it! This recipe is a slow cooker twist on an old favorite—chicken alfredo.

Cooking the chicken and pasta together blends the flavors and makes the chicken super tender while keeping the pasta perfectly al dente. It's important to add the Parmesan *after* the cream. If you add the cheese to the hot pasta it will break down and won't mix into the pasta well.

Using a slow cooker liner or lining your slow cooker with foil will make cleanup easy for this recipe!

Yield: **6 SERVINGS**

1 lb (454 g) fettuccini pasta, broken in half

2 chicken breasts, uncooked, chopped into 1-inch (3-cm) pieces

2½ cups (600 ml) chicken broth

4 cloves garlic, minced

½ tsp salt

½ tsp pepper

1½ cups (360 ml) heavy cream

½ cup (40 g) Parmesan cheese, grated

1 tbsp (4 g) fresh parsley

Place the fettuccini and the chicken in the slow cooker. Add the chicken broth, garlic, salt and pepper.

Cook on low for 2 hours or high for 1 hour, until the pasta is tender, stirring halfway through. Add the heavy cream, Parmesan cheese and parsley. Stir to combine and cover until the cream is heated through, about 15 minutes on low.

HOMEMADE LASAGNA

I love making this recipe: There is something about it that is so comforting and peaceful. This recipe is one of our favorites to take to friends and neighbors. It has helped console many broken hearts and strengthened weary bodies.

I made this recipe hundreds of times in order to perfect it! The balance of flavors and herbs in the sauce and filling is terrific. Another plus is that it is an all-in-one meal and requires no side dishes. I hope you love it as much as we do.

Using a slow cooker liner or lining your slow cooker with foil will make cleanup easy for this recipe!

Yield: **6 SERVINGS**

FOR THE SAUCE
½ cup (80 g) minced yellow onion

2 cloves garlic, minced

⅛ tsp red pepper flakes

1 (28-oz [794-g]) can crushed tomatoes

1 (15-oz [425-g]) can tomato sauce

1 (6-oz [170-g]) can tomato paste

¾ cup (180 ml) water

¼ cup (60 ml) heavy cream

1 tbsp (2 g) fresh basil

2 tsp (1 g) fresh oregano

FOR THE CHEESE FILLING
15 oz (425 g) ricotta cheese

1 cup (80 g) Parmesan cheese, grated

1 large egg

¾ cup (25 g) spinach, frozen or fresh, chopped

1 tsp salt

½ tsp pepper

FOR ASSEMBLY
1 lb (454 g) ground beef

8–10 regular lasagna noodles (do not use no-boil noodles)

3 cups (336 g) mozzarella cheese, shredded

2 tbsp (8 g) fresh parsley, chopped, for garnish

To make the sauce, in a large bowl, combine the onion, garlic, red pepper flakes, crushed tomatoes, tomato sauce, tomato paste, water, heavy cream, basil and oregano. Set aside.

To make the cheese filling, in a separate bowl, combine the ricotta, Parmesan cheese, egg, spinach, salt and pepper. Set aside.

To assemble, in a large skillet over medium heat, brown the ground beef, 5 to 7 minutes. Drain any excess grease, if necessary. Set aside.

Pour ½ cup (120 ml) of the sauce into the bottom of the slow cooker. Place a layer of lasagna noodles over the sauce. You will have to break a few to get them to cover the entire area of the slow cooker. Spread half of the cheese mixture evenly over the noodles. I find this works best if you use your hands. Sprinkle 1 cup (112 g) of the mozzarella cheese over the cheese mixture. Sprinkle ½ of the ground beef over the cheeses. Layer 2 to 3 cups (480 to 720 ml) of sauce over the ground beef and cheeses. Repeat the layering one more time. Finish with a final layer of lasagna noodles and the remainder of the sauce on top. Sprinkle the remaining cup (112 g) of mozzarella cheese on top of the lasagna.

Cook on high for 2 hours or low for 4 hours, until the pasta is tender. Sprinkle the chopped parsley on top for garnish.

*See image on page 148.

BEEF AND LAMB RAGU

Ragu is a traditional sauce that combines veggies and meat into a delicious pasta topping. I find the easiest way to get the fine, grated texture of the vegetables that the recipe calls for is to blend them briefly in a food processor. If you don't have a food processor, don't stress! You can easily use a cheese grater to get the same texture.

The long cooking time creates a smoothness to this sauce even though it has a lot of texture. I love the combination of meats and veggies. Magic happens as they all cook together, and you're left with a super flavorful sauce that packs a punch.

Yield: **6 SERVINGS**

1 tbsp (15 ml) olive oil

½ lb (227 g) ground beef

½ lb (227 g) ground lamb

1 medium yellow onion, grated

1 carrot, grated

1 celery stalk, grated

½ cup (120 ml) red wine

2 cups (480 ml) beef broth

1 (28-oz [794-g]) can crushed tomatoes

3 tbsp (50 g) tomato paste

2 tsp (10 ml) balsamic vinegar

1 tsp salt

¼ tsp red pepper flakes

1 bay leaf

1 tbsp (4 g) fresh parsley, minced

1 tbsp (2 g) fresh basil, minced

1 lb (454 g) cooked pasta, for serving

In a skillet, heat the olive oil over medium heat until shimmering. Add the ground beef and lamb and cook until browned, 5 to 7 minutes. Add the browned meat to the slow cooker along with the onion, carrot, celery, red wine, beef broth, crushed tomatoes, tomato paste, vinegar, salt, red pepper flakes and bay leaf.

Cook on high for 2 hours or low for 6 hours. Stir in the fresh parsley and basil. Serve over cooked pasta.

"BAKED" SLOW COOKER ZITI

While this recipe is obviously not baked, it's a nod to a classic pasta bake. It combines all the same flavors you would find in a lasagna but in a way that is easier to put together. This is one of my husband's favorite recipes and one of the few he will take for leftovers the next day! Everyone is sure to love this classic dish.

Using a slow cooker liner or lining your slow cooker with foil will make cleanup easy for this recipe!

Yield: **6 SERVINGS**

4 cloves garlic, minced

¼ tsp red pepper flakes

1 tsp salt, divided

1 (28-oz [794-g]) can crushed tomatoes

1 (15-oz [425-g]) can tomato sauce

1 (6-oz [170-g]) can tomato paste

¾ cup (180 ml) water

1 tsp basil, dried

½ tsp oregano, dried

1 cup (248 g) ricotta cheese

1 cup (240 ml) sour cream

1 cup (80 g) Parmesan cheese, grated

1 large egg

¾ cup (25 g) spinach, frozen or fresh, chopped fine

1 lb (454 g) ziti pasta, uncooked

2 cups (224 g) mozzarella cheese, shredded

2 tbsp (8 g) fresh parsley, chopped, for garnish

In a large bowl, combine the garlic, red pepper flakes, ½ teaspoon of salt, crushed tomatoes, tomato sauce, tomato paste, water, basil and oregano. Set aside.

In a separate bowl, combine the ricotta, sour cream, Parmesan cheese, egg, spinach and the remaining ½ teaspoon of salt. Set aside.

Pour half of the sauce mixture into the slow cooker. Pour half of the pasta into the sauce. Press the pasta down into an even layer in the sauce. Spread all of the ricotta mixture evenly over the noodles. Sprinkle 1 cup (112 g) of the mozzarella cheese over the ricotta mixture. Pour the remaining sauce over the layers already in the slow cooker. Add the remaining noodles to the sauce and press them into a single layer. Sprinkle the remaining 1 cup (112 g) of the mozzarella cheese on top of the pasta.

Cook on high for 2 hours or low for 4 hours, until the pasta is tender. Sprinkle the chopped parsley on top for garnish.

QUICK-COOK SAUSAGE PASTA

My family is crazy about sausage, so this is one of their favorite recipes! I prefer the texture of slow-cooked sausage over sausage cooked on the stovetop, so I'm happy to oblige their love with this recipe.

The simple flavors of this dish are perfect, and this sauce comes together so quickly in the slow cooker. It is important to cook the onions with the sausage in this recipe. Because the cook time is lower, that will ensure they are nice and tender and not still crisp.

Using a slow cooker liner or lining your slow cooker with foil will make cleanup easy for this recipe!

Yield: **6 SERVINGS**

1 tbsp (15 ml) olive oil

1 lb (454 g) ground Italian sausage, mild or spicy

½ cup (80 g) chopped yellow onion

24 oz (680 g) diced tomatoes

1 (6-oz [170-g]) can tomato paste

2½ cups (600 ml) water

2 tbsp (24 g) sugar

2 cloves garlic, minced

½ tsp salt

¼ tsp pepper

1 tbsp (4 g) fresh parsley

1 tbsp (2 g) fresh basil

2 tsp (1 g) fresh oregano

1 lb (454 g) penne pasta, uncooked

Grated Parmesan cheese, for garnish

In a skillet, heat the olive oil over medium heat until shimmering. Add the sausage to the skillet and cook until almost browned, about 5 minutes. Add the onion to the sausage and cook until the sausage is cooked through and the onion is translucent, 3 to 5 more minutes. Set aside.

Combine the diced tomatoes, tomato paste, water, sugar, garlic, salt, pepper, parsley, basil and oregano in the slow cooker. Nestle the penne and sausage and onion into the sauce.

Cook on high for 1 hour or low for 2 hours, until the pasta is tender. Garnish with Parmesan cheese.

LEMON-GARLIC PASTA

This pasta recipe takes almost no time to prepare and is absolutely bursting with flavor! I love anything creamy and anything lemon, so this is my go-to recipe when I want to satisfy those cravings.

The peas are a great addition to this recipe as well. They add some nice color and sweetness that pairs really well with the lemony sauce.

Using a slow cooker liner or lining your slow cooker with foil will make cleanup easy for this recipe.

Yield: **6 SERVINGS**

1 lb (454 g) fettuccini pasta, uncooked, broken in half

3 cups (720 ml) chicken broth

¼ cup (60 ml) lemon juice, freshly squeezed

4 cloves garlic, minced

½ tsp salt

½ tsp pepper

1½ cups (360 ml) heavy cream

1 cup (130 g) frozen peas

½ cup (40 g) Parmesan cheese, grated

1 tbsp (4 g) fresh parsley

Place the fettuccini in the slow cooker. Add the chicken broth, lemon juice, garlic, salt and pepper.

Cook on low for 2 hours or high for 1 hour, stirring halfway through, until the pasta is tender.

Add the heavy cream, peas, Parmesan cheese and parsley. Stir to combine and cover until the cream is heated through, about 15 minutes on low.

SPICY ROASTED RED PEPPER SAUCE

Spicy roasted red pepper sauce is a unique pasta topping you will love. Roasted red peppers are slightly sweet and they pair really well with the spice of the red pepper flakes. The tomato base of the sauce is hearty and supports the other flavors.

I like to serve this sauce over ravioli or tortellini because it complements the creamy, cheesy pasta. This recipe makes enough sauce for 1 pound (454 g) of pasta. Make sure you have some crusty bread on hand, too—you'll want to be able to clean up any sauce left on your plate!

Yield: **6 SERVINGS**

1 (16-oz [454-g]) jar roasted red peppers, including liquid

1 (28-oz [794-g]) can whole tomatoes

¾ cup (180 ml) water

2 tbsp (24 g) sugar

½ cup (80 g) chopped onion

2 cloves garlic, minced

½ tsp salt

2 tsp (3 g) red pepper flakes (see Note)

2 tsp (1 g) dried parsley

1 tsp dried basil

Combine the roasted red peppers and their liquid, the tomatoes, water, sugar, onion, garlic, salt, red pepper flakes, parsley and basil in the slow cooker.

Cook on high for 4 hours or low for 8 hours. Blend the sauce with an immersion blender, food processor or blender. Be very careful when doing this! Hot liquids expand.

Note: Using the full amount of red pepper flakes will make this dish very spicy. If you'd like a milder spice, use ½ teaspoon, or 1 teaspoon for a medium spice.

FARMERS MARKET TOMATO SAUCE

If you have a lot of fresh tomatoes, this recipe is calling your name! I love making this sauce in late summer when I have hundreds of tomatoes coming from my garden every week. The cooking times in this recipe are minimums. You can cook this for longer, but it's best to leave it on low if you are going to extend the cooking time.

How juicy your tomatoes are will determine the texture of your sauce. The sweetness of the sauce will also be determined by the kind of tomatoes you use. Any kind will work great, just taste test the sauce to ensure its flavor is where you want it to be. This sauce is great to serve over pasta, on pizza or as a dipping sauce for bread! This recipe makes enough sauce to coat 2 pounds (907 g) of pasta, or for eight personal pan–sized pizzas.

Yield: **8 SERVINGS**

8 cups (1.4 kg) tomatoes, chopped (see Note)

2 cloves garlic, smashed

I yellow onion, diced

I red bell pepper, diced

2 sprigs basil

I sprig oregano

2 sprigs parsley

3 tbsp (36 g) sugar

½ tsp red pepper flakes

I tsp salt

I (6-oz [170-g]) can tomato paste

I cup (240 ml) vegetable broth

Combine the tomatoes, garlic, onion, bell pepper, basil, oregano, parsley, sugar, red pepper flakes, salt, tomato paste and vegetable broth in the slow cooker.

Cook on high for 6 hours or low for 10 hours. When the sauce is finished cooking, blend it until it is smooth. You can use an immersion blender, food processor or blender. Be careful when blending the sauce! Hot liquids expand.

Note: I don't bother peeling my tomatoes (or really any vegetables for that matter), because as you are blending the sauce, the skin gets broken down and it doesn't detract from the texture of the sauce.

ACKNOWLEDGMENTS

First and foremost, I want to thank my husband, Andy. He has always been my number one supporter, confidant and friend. He is always one hundred percent confident in me and my abilities, even when I'm not. He is the one who encouraged me to write this cookbook and cheered me on along the way. From doing thousands of dishes to searching the store for fresh mint in February, he is always there when I need him.

I also want to thank my kids, Abram, Aspen and Ashton. They are still little but patient and helpful beyond their years. Writing and photographing a cookbook in the middle of a worldwide pandemic was not easy on any of us when school and babysitters suddenly went away. But they were quick to adapt and understanding when I had to work furiously during the baby's naptime instead of play and read books.

I'd like to thank my parents, family and friends. For helping me develop a love for food. For helping me turn that into a career. For reviewing recipes and photos for me at all hours of the day and night. For their positivity and encouragement.

I am so grateful for the team at Page Street Publishing and for the opportunity to write a cookbook that I'm so passionate about! Thank you to Madeline for her direction and patience with me as I learned how to write a cookbook and made a lot of mistakes. Thank you to Laura and Meg for their direction and expertise with the photography and design—the beauty of this book is because of them.

Lastly, thank you to my audience. The people who try the recipes, follow me on social media, share my recipes with their friends and know the names of my sheep. I so appreciate your support. I would not be here without you all.

ABOUT THE AUTHOR

Alli Kelley is the creator of the blog Longbourn Farm, where she shares simple homemade recipes. She loves helping her audience make their kitchens the heart of their homes. In addition to tried-and-true kitchen favorites, Alli shares practical farm and garden tips along with educational tidbits about farming and food production.

Her passion for and education in agriculture led her and her husband to eventually purchase their own small farm. There, she raises kids, sheep, chickens, bees, veggies and a handful of other animals. Her cooking incorporates simple, fresh ingredients she has on the farm.

INDEX